The Online Meeting Survival Guide

Learn how to use Facebook, Google Meet, Microsoft Teams, Skype and Zoom to enhance team communication.

By Paul W. Richards

ISBN: 9798643254980

DEDICATION

This book is dedicated to my wife, who as always, creates a space in the world where I can be productive, happy and loved.

CONTENTS

Part 1: How we Got Here

1   Online Collaboration is Now For Everyone   Pg 1

2   First, a Little Background: How Did We Get Here?   Pg 6

3   The Tools Were Just the Beginning: Essential Ideas for Online Communicators.   Pg 12

Part 2: Technical Review

4   Skype   Pg 17

5   Google Meet   Pg 32

6   Microsoft Teams   Pg 49

7   Zoom   Pg 64

8   Facebook   Pg 105

Part 3: Productivity Primer

9   Collaboration, is There a Downside?   Pg 118

10   Four Strategies for Hosting Productive Online Meetings   Pg 123

11   Video Communication Etiquette   Pg 128

12   Enhancing the Meeting Experience   Pg 134

13   Organizing Collaboration Channels   Pg 143

14   Priming for Productive Meetings   Pg 149

15   Hosting a Captivating Webinar   Pg 158

16   Innovations in Video Communications   Pg 161

17   Culture Pushes Us Forward   Pg 168

ACKNOWLEDGMENTS

I'd like to acknowledge all of the amazing people who I have collaborated with online to make this book a possibility. This includes Francesca Kennedy and Tobi Elkin, my amazing editors. There are too many people to name here individually, but you know who you are.

1 ONLINE COMMUNICATIONS TECHNOLOGY
IT'S FOR EVERYONE NOW

January 2020…

Innovations in online communications were already expanding the horizons of voice and video collaboration when the global pandemic COVID-19 started. In a matter of months, the world's largest work-from-home experiment of the information age was launched. Adaptation being the key to survival, suddenly everyone from managers to mothers, science teachers to students, and governors to grandparents were forced to venture into the brave new universe of online communication.

Let's step back to that moment in time. It's 2020…unless you've been living in a cave, the COVID-19 pandemic has changed the way you do business, attend school, participate in group affiliations like churches and clubs, and even how you stay close to friends and family. From consumer video conferencing to business collaboration and productivity, necessity truly is the mother of invention. In the midst of rapid change, online communication has landed firmly at the center of this "new normal" for everyone. Remote workers of all kinds and isolated families across the globe now rely on online voice and video to stay connected.

Even though an internet connection and a computer are all that's needed for crash-course in video conferencing, it's not always that simple. All but veteran techies can feel like "digital migrants" as they work their way through the minefields of their first online gatherings and conferences, facing obstacles like dropped connections and video with garbled audio while learning to creatively pantomime "I can't hear you."

I've written this book to help readers, skilled and novice alike, master online technologies so they can focus optimistically on discovering the many opportunities this greater reliance on online communication can offer. Through my online course, and the chapters in this book, readers have the chance to learn about the best tools available, hone their online communication skills, and push their overall productivity forward into the 21st century. As we witness the use of online video communication accelerates to mass adoption worldwide, with it comes endless opportunities for those with a keen eye for emerging trends.

What do you get when you combine Zoom video conferencing with school field trips? Boom! A new educational business is born. FieldTripZoom is an actual company that has become so popular, they have to use live streaming to accommodate some of their larger events because they outgrew Zoom.

Merge video conferencing and live streaming? How about a new talk show or a podcast with audiences that potentially rival that of television or cable networks? My personal favorite is spiritual sharing and online worship groups, hosted by small churches that have found an even larger community than they originally realized. More realistic perhaps for most is the realization of increased productivity through expanded communication and collaboration opportunities.

This book will not only help you discover how to curate your online communication technology, it will encourage you to venture out and create your online specialty. I'm going to show you the strategies and best practices you need to harness the power of all the latest video communication tools to free *you* to develop fresh ideas to apply to your unique vision.

I know, change can be uncomfortable, but the future *always* holds a silver lining for forward thinkers. For example, the widespread adoption of video communications has the power to reduce travel which is positive in terms of reducing the world's carbon footprint.

That's good for combating global warming. There are also many win-win business scenarios, like a more diversified and productive workforce. And most employers welcome the opportunity to reduce the cost of office space by expanding to a larger remote workforce. This change may wind up saving companies hundreds of millions of dollars each year on office leases, security, and other related costs.

For many, today's "new normal" involves a significant amount of telecommuting and it's likely to stay that way for the foreseeable future. Even before the pandemic, expanding the number of remote workers was already a trend supported by many top corporate executives. A recent Gartner Organization study (Gartner, April 2020) showed that 74 percent of chief financial officers (CFOs) surveyed expected to move previously on-site employees to remote work *permanently* post COVID-19. Many participating CFOs hinted that remote work may become more of the norm than the exception as companies look to cut commercial real estate costs and better safeguard their workforce from communicable illnesses.

At the same time, as employers look to reap these potential benefits, workers too are finding a better work-life balance by leveraging the collaboration tools that allow them to work from home. Remote employees can instantly eliminate the time spent commuting to and from work. This time-savings may translate to more quality time with family and friends, and that just might make employees happier and more productive in the long run. And that's a boon for business and family life.

For companies looking to improve their bottom lines, happy people tend to be more productive. A 2015 study at the University of Warwick (Warwick, ac.uk, 2015) found that happy employees are, on average, 12 percent more productive than unhappy employees. For most workers, an improved work-life balance increases happiness and by extension, improves productivity. The shift to remote work may lead to happier people living in a more productive and environmentally friendly society.

Businesses in turn can enjoy increased employee productivity. Now that's a win-win.

This book will review top video conferencing and online communication solutions, keeping in mind the business goal of increased worker productivity. Where we sit today, having experienced a global pandemic, we find the adoption of technology has advanced what might have taken years into a matter of months by sheer necessity. Businesses around the world were forced to reexamine and reinvent their communications logistics to facilitate all their employees working from home for extended periods, a trend unlikely to reverse anytime soon. The Genie is out of the box, but as I mentioned, that needn't be a bad thing.

The video conferencing technologies this book examines include Google Hangouts/Meet, Facebook Rooms, Skype, Microsoft Teams, and Zoom. The collaboration technologies this book will reference include Google Chat, the G Suite, Teams, Discord, and Slack. While many companies standardize with just one or two of these solutions, everyone needs to develop a basic familiarity with each of the world's top online communication tools because you never know which ones an employer will use to do business. It's important to remain agile, adaptable, and ready to adopt new technologies applications quickly. Not to worry, these tools are easy to learn, and you'll pick them up quickly.

Looking ahead, after using some of these tools, it's natural to develop a favorite. I encourage this. After all, it's *your* online productivity. For the times you're the host of an event, you're in the driver's seat and get to choose the tool that offers all the features you need to accomplish your goals. But, for the times you need to use a tool of someone else's choosing, I'll help you become familiar with the communications platforms available today.

Once you've mastered the tools of online collaboration, you'll learn about the social side of meetings. I'll teach you how to tune up a known super skill – the power of listening. I'll also teach you how to head-off unproductive online meetings or collaboration projects. In essence, you'll learn how to make the most of your online *time* using online communications.

There's no avoiding it, as you venture into the world of online meetings, you're bound to be invited, or compelled to use a variety of new online tools. My goal is that when you're finished reading this book, you'll be prepared to assess and navigate all the amazing online meeting solutions from the top providers... the ones used by the most forward-thinking businesses. Then it's up to you to decide which of these tools is best for you and your team.

Are you ready to get started? Let's cut to the chase and dig into the fundamentals online communicators need to know.

2 FIRST A LITTLE BACKGROUND. HOW DID WE GET HERE?

In a matter of seconds, an online search will find hundreds of communication applications you can install on your smartphone, computer, or tablet. Each service promises to be the best, most intuitive solution for online communication with family, friends, and business partners. It's never been easier or more convenient to send a message, share a picture, or connect face-to-face with other people around the world. But it wasn't always this way. The communications tools of today are the result of an evolution of technological innovations that spans several decades.

The earliest online chat messaging and email applications, like AOL, MindSpring, and Yahoo, were initially only available to small groups of computer owners. Try imagining a time when sending an instant message or email between two computers was new and exciting. Once upon a time, the only way to send an *instant* message (IM) was by telegram, Telex, or fax. Are you old enough to remember? Likely, millennials and Gen Z have never even heard of these methods.

Instant messages (IMs) and email represented the first wave of online communications. Instant messaging predates the internet and unlike many other technologies, IMs and email remain important today. These two methods of communication were important building blocks of the "technology stacks" (lists of services built to run on a single application) for online communication and collaboration. Like an old-fashioned phone call, instant messaging and email which essentially function the same, with a few added bells and whistles, have been modernized but never replaced.

The internet (a global system of interconnected computer networks) has transformed the global communications landscape more than any other technology. In 1993, two-way communications on the internet represented only one percent of all communications. By 2000, that number increased to 51 percent and by 2007, that number had climbed to 97 percent (Hilbert, 2011). When the world's communications moved online, many new business opportunities emerged. From social media to digital advertising, economies around the world have flourished as benefactors of this massive movement.

As the internet expanded, Software as a Service (SaaS), and cloud computing, (off-premise data warehousing) emerged. SaaS is when a provider hosts an application, making them available on-demand by subscription to customers over the internet, instead of having to download them to their local or network drive. SaaS examples include the Google G Suite, Slack, Office 365, Dropbox, and Zoom. Providers such as Amazon, Google, and Microsoft have helped companies deliver SaaS via cloud computing technology, enabling them to offer a variety of new and powerful front-end software applications. Delivering software via the cloud has made businesses more agile and scalable.

For the consumer, cloud solutions eliminate many barriers to entry where personal and enterprise software are concerned. The migration to the cloud allows providers to leave expensive, one-time purchases in the history books while offering customers more affordable monthly subscriptions. This also allows consumers to adopt products more rapidly and in ever-increasing numbers. As a result of cloud computing, SaaS providers can update their products with unprecedented speed, allowing them to keep up with changing consumer demands. The flexibility of cloud-based solutions has changed consumer expectations. Providers now must streamline the deployment of new products and services to offer seamless device cross-compatibility to compete. Managing software solutions in the cloud also enable companies to *combine* their services to form multipurpose platforms like, for example, creating a Google Meet integration directly within Gmail. Furthermore, Application Programming Interfaces (APIs) give companies the ability to integrate third-party software into these services for limitless customization and the development of truly unique software solutions.

Concurrently with SaaS developments, both IM and email continued to grow in popularity as businesses went "paperless." Then, in 2003, Skype video conferencing launched and quickly became one of the first video solutions to enjoy worldwide adoption. Skype featured the ability to host audio and video communications between as many as 25 callers which was a game-changer. Skype's innovation is also historically significant due to its innovation user-friendliness. By 2004, Skype had logged 1.5 million downloads and 100,000 concurrent users (Skype, 2012).

Following seven successful years of growth, Microsoft acquired Skype in 2011. Two years after the purchase, Google entered the market with "Hangouts." Hangouts was Google's first video communication tool and it was designed to run inside any web browser on a SaaS model. By the time Hangouts launched, Google's Gmail had 500 million users, and Hangouts, built directly into the Gmail platform, became instantly accessible to a massive user base.

Google soon added new services to the platform, integrating Gmail with other web-based services such as Google Calendar, Google Drive, and a suite of document creation tools (Docs, Sheets, and Slides). Gmail has achieved astounding growth, and it all began by offering free email services. Google has used the email service. Google has used the service as the gateway for over 1.5 billion users to access Hangouts. To put this into perspective, in January of 2012, there were 350 million Gmail users. By October of 2018, just six years later, Gmail reported over 1.5 billion users.

Microsoft's Skype and Google's Hangouts have consistently led the online communications industry since the beginning of the 21st century. Microsoft and Google each offer a similar suite of online collaboration tools. In 2006, Google released its "G Suite" subscription service, a central cloud-based workspace for collaboration, storage, and communications. Five years later in 2011, Microsoft released its cloud-based productivity suite, "Office 365." By 2019, Microsoft reported its

Office 365 product had reached 180 million users. In 2020, Google's G Suite user base had surpassed two billion.

Since acquiring Skype in 2003, Microsoft has seen many iterations of video conferencing services. Microsoft continued to redesign its online communications tools for business purposes with Skype for Business, a retooling of Microsoft Lync. Then, in 2017, Microsoft announced it would phase out Skype for Business and replace it with Microsoft "Teams."

Teams combines the best elements of Skype's video conferencing solutions with a more robust team-based approach to online communications that includes threaded conversations and channel-based project collaboration. These changes essentially mark the division of Microsoft's conferencing solutions into a consumer version of Skype with Teams as the main video conferencing solution for business.

Google's video communication solutions have also gone through significant changes. Google announced that it would phase out Google Hangouts in favor of Google Meet starting in 2020.

As Google and Microsoft continued to expand their cloud-based productivity offerings, many other players in the professional video conferencing space also flourished. These include Bluejeans, GoToMeeting, WebEx, and Zoom among others. GoToMeeting and WebEx were early cloud-based video conferencing solutions that helped to end an era of expensive hardware-based video conferencing solutions. Cisco launched WebEx in 2007 a few years after Citrix debuted GoToMeeting in 2004.

In 2011, a former WebEx engineer named Eric Yuan formed yet another video conferencing company called Zoom. Zoom launched in 2013, as the first video conferencing solution design featuring a video-first approach with a user-friendly meeting control bar. Zoom gradually became known as the affordable alternative to its professional online communications competitors with pricing set at $9.99 per month per user. In 2015 for example, a GoToMeeting license cost $39.99 per user per month, while Zoom pricing was less than $10 per month for a comparable product.

But it wasn't just its price that would make Zoom the dominant video conferencing software provider by 2020. Zoom's reputation for ease of use and reliability helped grow its market share, as more companies and individual users switched over from alternatives. In the tech industry, an application like Zoom is called "sticky" because once users try it, they stick with it and share it with others.

 Sticky Zoom was ideally positioned when the world's largest work-from-home project exploded brought on by a global pandemic. Zoom's "freemium" license model allows people to start using the product free for one-to-one calls while enticing them to upgrade to paid plans to access additional features. When the third or fourth caller enters a meeting without a paid account hosting the meeting, the meeting is restricted by a 40-minute time limit. Zoom's product positioning and "freemium" model has taken the world by storm. Currently, a Zoom professional account starts at $14.99 for groups of nine users or less and $19.99 for groups with more than 10 users.

In response to Zoom's market dominance, in April 2020 Google decided to make it's Meet video conferencing service free for Gmail users with *no* time restrictions for up to 100 meeting participants. In the same month, Google said it's Meet product added three million new users daily, growing by a factor of 30x during the coronavirus pandemic. Not to be left out, during this time Facebook improved its existing Messenger product to support up to 50 video callers with a new product launch called Rooms (*Fortune*, 2020).

In general, however, online communications have seen relatively slow but steady growth in user adoption over the past few decades. More recently, the benefits of shared online workspaces and low monthly user costs have pushed many organizations to the cloud with record growth in adoption. While early technology adopters certainly helped spread the value of online communications, nothing could've pushed the industry forward more rapidly than mandated shelter in place orders around the world which forced millions of people to work from home. This immediate and total need for efficient online communication and effective collaboration is driving innovation to every corner of the modern workforce.

3 The Tools Were Just the Beginning: Essential Ideas for Online Communicators

Suffice to say, communications have changed dramatically in the 21st century. The smartphone has made instantaneous access to information commonplace and small internet-connected devices such as tablets have put instant messaging, voice, video, and data access into the hands of millions in a relatively short period. Communications have evolved rapidly but with so many innovations happening simultaneously, there are few clear guidelines on how individuals and teams can best use these technologies to become more productive. At the same time, we have experienced a cultural shift, the world of work is adapting to deliver flexible, user-friendly communications services.

Daniel Pink, the author of *To Sell Is Human*, has uncovered eye-opening research that can help us to better understand the transformations happening in the modern workplace. Pink's research shows that on average, 40 percent of most workers' time is spent "persuading, convincing, and influencing others." Pink's first-of-its-kind research shows that modern workers have been asked to develop skills that cross traditional departmental boundaries to increase productivity. Pink argues that a "broad rethinking of sales as we know it" can help explain the paradigm shift in modern communication. Pink goes on to note that while only one in nine jobs in the United States are in direct sales, the other eight in nine jobs involve what he describes as "non-sales selling" (Pink, 2019).

Modern Workforce Transformation

Sales Person

Non-Sales Selling

40% of time spent on the job dedicated to
persuading, convincing or influencing others.

Collaboration between multiple business units both inside and outside of organizations is key to this modern workforce transformation. Pink notes two fast-growing industries, education, and medicine, are deeply involved in "moving people." These industries have renamed entire sectors, i.e., "telehealth" and "distance learning" in support of this growing movement. Modern communications technology has helped facilitate and speed these changes.

Telehealth is the fastest growing area of the healthcare system, according to the American Medical Association (AMA) (AMA, 2019). In the field of education, a study by the Online Learning Consortium (OLC), published *before* the COVID-19 outbreak reports that distance learning had been growing every year for 16 years (OLC, 2018). After COVID-19, educators from all walks of life and generations have had to reinvent and reimagine their educational processes to adapt to some form of distance learning using online communication tools.

Both of these industries rely heavily on effective communication. When communication between multiple business units is essential, online communications become the foundation that connects distributed teams whether they're located across the hall or the globe. These same communications tools have allowed the education and healthcare sectors to deliver their services remotely over the internet. This dynamic, in turn, has enabled them to find new emerging segments within their industries allowing their teams to build ancillary services into their business model that did not exist previously.

For example, doctors can save patients the hassle of coming into the office with simple follow up visits that can be conducted over a video conference. These new emerging segments help make their organizations more profitable and diversified. The virtualization of healthcare and educational services has increased the number of services these organizations can offer and therefore the number of people they can serve. As a result, each of these industries is now able to generate thousands of new jobs every year.

How many more industries will be transformed by online communications technology? Yet another example is how the COVID-19 pandemic has forced the trillion-dollar event planning industry to move completely online. My book *The Virtual Ticket* (2020) reviews the transformation of the events industry that was forced to postpone or cancel in-person events as a result of COVID-19. The entire events sector continues to rethink its role and go-to-market strategies – it must adapt in light of the pandemic.

As event managers attempt to sell virtual tickets, their events can become even more profitable and diversified online. Emerging opportunities include personalized health and wellness, as instructors, coaches, and other providers can go all-in on video communications. How about an online yoga class with a celebrity? A writing course with a leading author? Or, a cake decorating class with a pastry chef? Providers like MasterClass were already in the market with virtual offerings before the pandemic hit. What's changing now is how it's not just about established organizations; people everywhere are uncovering the power of video communications. Consequently, it's becoming the norm to be searching for that "secret sauce" and unique value-add that communications technologies can help them deliver.

Online tools can help enhance the way we communicate when we apply traditional communication principles to the modern meeting. Even though the way humans communicate today is drastically different from the way humans communicated even just a decade ago, demonstrating a robust mission, cultivating mutual respect, and authentic communication remain the keys to success. Online communication technologies allow you to extend the reach of your organization's communications and strengthen your offerings. So, amid seismic and rapid technological changes, it's worth remembering that ongoing, effective communication and relationship-building remain the linchpins of business success.

Taking this idea, a step further, Joseph Pine, the author of *The Experience Economy* argues that consumers value goods and services more when businesses design specific experiences that accompany the goods and services they're promoting and selling. In Chapter 11, we'll explore the process of repositioning your unique sales value through productive online meetings that enhance your customers' experience with your product or service. There are simple steps that you can take meeting attendees through to have more meaningful conversations and thought-provoking dialogue on your subject matter. So, look to the latter part of the book for guidance on this.

 Let's get started...in the next section, you'll learn about the most important feature sets available on Skype, Google Meet, Microsoft Teams, Zoom, and Facebook Rooms. As you learn the intricacies of each video communication solution, think about your aspirations for communications. Think about the tools and how you can apply them to the unique needs of your business.

Part 2: The Technical Review

Now that you've got a good idea of how today's video conferencing and collaboration tools were first developed, we'll look at some of the most popular solutions, their capabilities, and learn how to use them most effectively. Let's start with one of the most popular solutions, Skype.

4 SKYPE

Now that you've got a good idea of how today's video conferencing and collaboration tools were first developed and evolved, we will take a look at some of the most popular solutions, take a deep dive into their capabilities and learn how to use them most effectively. Let's start with one of the most popular solutions, Skype.

Topic/Feature	Details
Date Launched	2003. Purchased by Microsoft in 2001.
Price	Free. Credits and subscriptions are required for phone calling.
Meeting Participants	Maximum of 100. More available with Microsoft Teams.
Estimated Monthly Users	300 Million.
Screen Share &	Yes. Video recordings saved in the cloud and

Recording	available for download within 30 days.
Instant Messaging	Yes. Unlimited file transfer sizes

Can we Skype? The name of the service has become ubiquitously synonymous as *the* action verb for video chats. Skype's ability to connect people around the world has made history in the video communication space. Since its 2003 release, Skype's brought millions of friends and families together in a simple, straightforward interface. Microsoft, always on the lookout for innovative solutions, acquired Skype in 2011 and quickly integrated it into Microsoft Office, later known as Microsoft Office 365.

Four years after the acquisition, Microsoft launched "Skype for Business," which improved on its existing "Lync" business communication software by expanding integration capabilities. With Skype for Business, users experienced Outlook and other Office software directly with Skype for Business IM, voice, and video features by clicking directly on a contact (recipient) to initiate conversations or schedule meetings. Simply put, Skype for Business made Lync more useful.

Skype for Business targeted professional users at a cost, while Skype (for personal use) remained free. By comparison, while Skype permitted conferencing with up to 25 users, Skype for Business managed up to 250. Skype for Business also offered dedicated video conferencing rooms. These "Room Systems" offered video collaboration experiences which included voice, video, and content collaboration via one Skype login.

Lync, Skype for Business, and eventually Microsoft Teams

In a nutshell, Lync was Microsoft's original business video communication solution. It morphed into Skype for Business similar to the way Google rebranded Hangouts into its Meet product. In the most recent iteration, Microsoft integrated Skype for Business into Office 365, its cloud-based productivity solution, Skype remains the most popular option for personal use as Microsoft Teams combines Skype's exceptional video communications features with Office 365. Teams also includes collaboration features similar to platforms such as "Slack" (released in 2013) and others. We'll look more closely at Teams and solutions like Slack in a bit. Let's circle back and take a deeper dive into Skype.

A Closer Look at Skype

With Skype, users can connect up to 50 meeting participants in High Definition (HD) video quality. Skype video calls include intuitive screen sharing and messaging features that complement the meeting experience. The Skype messaging feature allows users to chat, share pictures, and use "@" mentions to get other users' attention. Skype's messaging platform can be used independently from its video conferencing mode. While it's often used as a chat solution, users can transition to a video call whenever necessary.

Video Recordings

Skype calls can be recorded for review later. Start a Skype recording by pressing the button in the bottom right-hand side of the screen and select **Start Recording**. Skype recordings are stored in the cloud for 30 days and are available for download directly through the Skype software. Once your meeting is over, click the **More Options** button and select **Save As** to download the recording onto your computer's hard drive.

Phone Calling

Skype to Skype audio calls have always been free. But Skype phone calling also enables you to reach people who aren't online. Calling someone via a phone number requires Skype credits. Users can also sign up to receive a Skype phone number if they don't already have one. Skype phone numbers allow users to pay a flat fee for unlimited phone calls. In the U.S., for example, this service costs $6.50 per month. Skype phone calling has many of the features traditional phone service providers offer such as call forwarding and voicemail.

Skype Translator

Skype Translator is an exciting new feature that performs live voice translations. With Translator, users around the world can communicate with each other while Skype translates the conversations between each language. It works by "listening" to audio from one side of the conversation and then translating it into the native language of the person on the other end of the video conference and vice-versa. In this way, users can have conversations with people who speak foreign languages without a human translator present.

As of early 2020, Skype was able of translating the following languages via voice: English, Spanish, French, German, Chinese (Mandarin), Italian, Portuguese (Brazilian), Arabic, and Russian, with more languages, planned. Skype also supports over 60 languages via text translation. Text translations translate spoken languages into text that appears on the screen for meeting participants to read on the other side in their native languages.

Getting Started with Skype

Over the years, Skype has made its intuitive software available for use on smartphones, tablets, computers, TVs, and the Xbox One. In this section of the book, learn how to get started with Skype.

Registering

First, you need to register your Skype account. To register, visit Skype.com.

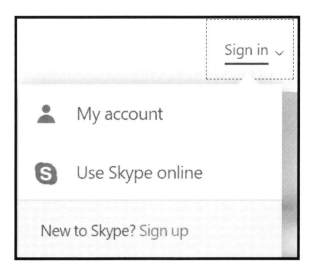

1. In the top-right corner of the web page click the option to **Sign in** to view **Sign up**.
2. Choose the option to login via your Microsoft or Facebook accounts or use your email address to sign up for a new Skype account. Signing in with an existing Facebook account allows you to connect with friends on Facebook to share, comment, like, and see updates from your Friends list.

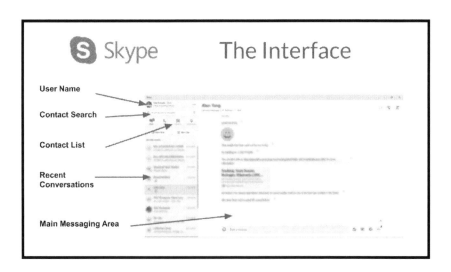

3. Once you're logged in successfully, you can easily make a video or voice call with your list of friends online.

Creating your "Contacts" or "Friends" list is the first step to success on Skype. This is why integrating a Facebook account is a great idea. You must permit Skype to access your Friends list, public profile, news feed, status updates, hometown, photos, website, videos, and other personal information to use Skype with Facebook. If you're not comfortable with this, don't connect your Facebook account. You can still add contacts to Skype without a Facebook account by searching for contacts in the Skype Directory.

Downloading Skype

After creating your account, Skype will prompt you to buy credits. You can skip this step if you don't need to use Skype for phone (voice only) calls.

Mac Users: Download the Mac OS version of Skype. Select the latest Mac software version and once downloaded, double-click the file and drag the icon into the application folder. Then, access Skype from the application folder, open the application, create a username and password, and log in.

Windows Users: Download the Windows version of Skype by double-clicking a downloaded thumbnail to start the installation process. When the installation is complete, open Skype, create a username and password and log in.

Android and iOS: The Skype apps for Android and iOS mobile devices are similar. Download the Android version from the Google Play Store or the iOS app from the Apple App Store. After downloading, launch the app, create a username and password, and log in.

When logging in for the first time, the application will ask you to customize your language, camera, audio, and profile picture settings.

The Skype Directory

Skype will easily connect you with millions of people around the world. But first, you'll need to add them as contacts. If you signed in with Facebook, contacts would display on the left side of the page, as shown below.

Adding a New Contact

1. Click into the Search box in the upper left corner of the main page and start typing the email address, username, first or last name, or phone number of the person you're looking for. As you type, if the person has already registered for Skype or if they're in your contacts, their name will appear in the contacts list.
2. Select a contact from the contact list to start a conversation by IM or to make a phone or video call.

Filter the Skype search bar by clicking the **People, Messages,** or **Group** buttons below the search bar. Messages and Groups are unique to your Skype user ID and will only show results if you have a Message or Group that matches your search query. When you want to add someone to your contact list, it's a good idea to ask for their Skype ID as this will help narrow the search results. You may find multiple users with the same name during a search, but a Skype user ID is always unique. You can also identify contacts by the picture associated with their account if they have one. Alternatively, you can also search using a Microsoft email address.

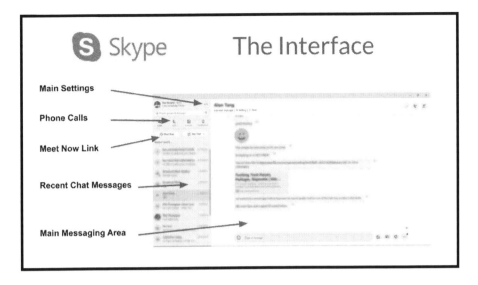

Connecting to Call, Message, and Video Conference

Skype requires both parties involved to accept a connection. The first time you try to connect with someone, Skype sends them a request and when they accept, they're added to your contacts list and you're free to chat, call, or video conference.

Sending a Message to a Skype Contact

1. Select a **Contact** from the list.
2. Click into the text box at the bottom of the screen, type your message, and press **Enter**.

Use this messaging area to share videos, files, and photos. Skype has no file sharing size limits which makes it a great feature for collaboration projects.

To call a friend, click the **Audio Call/**button above the Contact List. This button is also found in the upper right corner of the Skype window. To start a video chat, click the **Video Call/**button next to the name of the contact.

Meet Now

One of the easiest ways to launch a Skype meeting with anyone in the world is with "Meet Now" a feature that creates an ad-hoc meeting room you can invite others into. This feature displays on a button above the contact list:

1. Click **Meet Now** to get started.

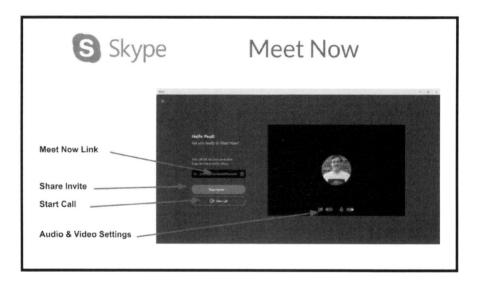

Meet Now instantly launches a new meeting window with a URL you can send via email or text.

Copy and send this URL to anyone in the world and they can easily join your meeting via Skype application or using any web browser.

Calls to Landlines or Mobile Phones

The price of a Skype phone call depends on the location of the receiver. You'll need Skype credits to make calls; option to automatically buy credits when your balance is low. To manage your credits:

1. Sign into your account.
2. Select your **Name** in the upper left-hand corner of the screen. Your remaining balance appears next to your name.
3. Double-click the dollar amount.

4. Click to buy the amount of credit you want and follow the instructions.

Skype Settings

1. To access Skype settings, click your profile picture and select the **Settings** cog. Here's a description of each setting:

Account Profile Settings: Account information, including your profile picture, username, and password.

General Settings: Global settings such as the application language and accessibility settings, including translation options.

Appearance Settings: Adjust the color scheme and choose among the applications' compact modes.

Audio and Video Settings: Adjust and monitor your webcam and microphone settings here.

Call Settings: Manage Caller ID, Call Forwarding and Voicemail.

Messaging Settings: Adjust things like the text size of incoming messages and more.

Notification Settings: Adjust the number of items Skype will notify you about. There's even a "Do not Disturb" setting.

Contact Settings: Manage privacy settings and banned contacts.

Help/Feedback: Confirm which version of Skype you have, review the current status of Skype, and find links to additional resources here.

Your First Skype

Before your first video conference, Skype will prompt you to select Audio and Video Settings and check your microphone and webcam devices to determine if they're functioning properly.

1. First, check to make sure your speakers are working by clicking the **Test Audio** button. If you hear audio playing, the speakers are working. If you don't hear audio, you may need to select a new speaker.
2. Next, make sure that your microphone works. If it is, you'll see level indicators move when you speak. If you don't see them, you may need to select a different mic from the drop-down menu.
3. Finally, check to make sure that your camera works. You can see yourself in a small window if it works. If not, review your camera settings.

Tips to Optimize Your Skype Experience

Network Assessment

It's always a good idea to check the bandwidth of your internet connection before hosting an important Skype meeting. Bandwidth is the amount of data your computer can send and receive to and from your internet service provider each second. To determine the bandwidth of your internet connection, search "internet speed test" on Google which . performs this test directly from the search results. If your video quality is poor, it may be a bandwidth issue.

A bandwidth test results in two numbers – your upload speed and your download speed. Download speeds are used to request information from the internet. Upload speeds are used to send information from your computer. Bandwidth speeds are generally measured in megabits per second. Ideally, you want at least 2-5 megabits per second of upload and download speed to operate a High-Definition (HD) videoconference.

Test with Small Group

Always test your system before an important meeting on Skype. Set up a "test" Skype call with a friend or two. Check the signal strength of your WiFi connection if you're using WiFi with a laptop. When possible, it's best to hard-wire your computer to an ethernet connection.

Right Equipment

The good news about Skype is that it requires very little technology. Start with an updated computer, access to a steady internet connection, a USB-connected webcam, and a microphone.

While it's commonplace to have a webcam and microphone already built into your laptop, you may want to upgrade to higher quality webcam and microphone accessories. Why? It makes a *big* difference in how you look and sound.

Host and record a meeting with a friend to experiment with how you look and sound on a Skype call. With Skype, it's easy to record a call and review the video footage. Try various backgrounds to appear more professional. How about a bookshelf instead of a blank white wall? Was your appearance dim or grainy? Turn on more lights or place additional lighting in the room so that the camera can see you.

Sound quality improves by using a headset microphone. If you're using Skype to record video content for YouTube, upgrades become extremely important. When using Skype to record a podcast, for example, you may want to invest in a high-quality USB microphone and a pair of headphones.

Webcams feature pan, tilt, and zoom functionality. The HuddleCamHD Pro webcam, for example, enables you to zoom in and pan around your room to make dynamic presentations. This webcam includes a remote control that enables you to zoom in and frame subjects to display them more clearly during video calls. Upgrading your video equipment will improve your video conferencing experience and is a good investment.

Skype Security

Skype's security policy requires that all users have a unique Skype ID which is used for authentication when combined with a username and password, or another authentication method. Microsoft manages its authentication servers to verify that all parties in a Skype call have authentic and unique IDs. Skype Messages are also encrypted for an additional layer of security. Some security flaws in the Skype system have been exposed over the years but Microsoft has implemented patches to resolve these issues. Learn more about Skype Security at https://support.skype.com/en/skype/all/privacy-security/.

5 GOOGLE MEET

Topic/Feature	Details
Date Launched	It started in 2013 as "Hangouts." Rebranded as "Meet" in 2020.
Price	Freemium. G Suite subscription unlocks all features.
Meeting Participants	Maximum of 250. 100,000 via live streaming option.
Estimated Monthly Users	100 Million. Gmail has over 1.5 billion users; G Suite has two billion users.
Screen Share	Yes. Supports video sharing via Chrome.
Online Workspace	G Suite. Complete cloud-based collaboration workspace.
Unique Feature #1	Cloud/Browser-based platform. No downloads required.
Unique Feature #2	G Suite Integration. Easy to use for G Suite subscribers.
Unique Feature #3	Live Streaming. Easily accommodates up to 100,000 viewers via live streaming.

Today, video communication has become an integral part of how we work. Indeed, for some, it is the *only* way to work. Even with so many video communication platforms available today, Google Hangouts (now Google Meet) is one of the most popular choices, almost by default. Google Meet is a powerful part of a larger set of tools. Meet is incredibly easy to use because it's integrated directly into Gmail and the G Suite. For many people, Google is a gateway to their online experience and its G Suite has become their workspace for online collaboration.

In 2016, Google announced that Gmail had passed one billion active users. Today that number is beyond 1.5 billion. Each user has free access to Google Chat for messaging and Google Meet for video conferencing. In addition to Gmail, Google offers video conferencing, messaging, and collaboration tools that are extremely helpful for boosting business productivity from directly within the G Suite platform.

The G Suite is a complete online workspace with popular applications such as Google Drive (file storage), Google Docs (documents), Google Slides (presentations), and Google Sheets (spreadsheets). Google's G Suite starts at just $6 per user, per month which offers any size business access to its set of online collaboration tools without prohibitive costs. With so many people actively using Google services, it's no wonder Google Meet has become one of the most popular video conferencing tools. Below is a look at services G Suite customers can access for low monthly fees.

Feature:	Basic	Business	Enterprise
Price	$6/User/Mo	$12/User/Mo	$25/User/Mo
Gmail	✓	✓	✓
Meet	✓	✓	✓

Chat	✓	✓	✓
Calendar	✓	✓	✓
Drive	30GB cloud storage	Unlimited cloud storage*	Unlimited cloud storage*
Docs	✓	✓	✓
Sheets	✓	✓	✓
Slides	✓	✓	✓
Forms	✓	✓	✓
Sites	✓	✓	✓
Keep	✓	✓	✓
Current	✓	✓	✓
App Scripts	✓	✓	✓
Cloud Search	✖	✓	✓
Data Loss Prevention	✖	✖	✓
*Unlimited for groups with over 5 users.			
**Pricing subject to change. Accurate as of May 2020.			

What is Google Meet?

Google Meet is perhaps the most accessible video conferencing tool on the market because it's a tool that's nested into a service that many people already use – Gmail.

The fact that Google's online communication tools are deeply integrated makes for a powerful user experience. Google's Gmail is primarily used for email and, like Skype, users can create a shortlist of contacts they can instant message, video conference with, or chat. Consistent users of Gmail have expanded their email communications to include voice, video, and screen sharing with Google Meet.

Google's "Chat" service offers threaded conversations that users organize into channels, similar to offerings by Teams, Slack, and Discord. Google's G Suite users find they collaborate quite effectively inside of a shared online workspace with only a short learning curve. Online workspaces have become de rigueur for connecting and collaborating with remote teams everywhere through a simple, accessible, and seamless interface.

Google G Suite: Google's G Suite is an online workspace built especially for online communications. Each G Suite user receives a single email address to log in to all of the G Suite tools. G Suite document creation tools such as Docs, Sheets, and Slides are easily shared and organized among remote teams around the world. G Suite also handles file storage on Google Drive, collaboration projects via Google Chat, and video conferencing with Google Meet. The G Suite also includes a detailed administration console for IT managers who customize the system to their organization's specific needs.

Google Hangouts: A web-based video chat and messaging service that Google had integrated into Gmail and is no longer supporting. Google announced that it will shelve Hangouts in 2020 and replace it with Meet.

Google Chat: Google Chat is built into Gmail. It provides instant messaging with a user's contacts. A new Chat feature allows you to organize collaboration projects into channels called rooms where users can chat in threaded discussions.

Google Meet: Google Meet is the official replacement for Google Hangouts; you can integrate the free video conferencing tool into the G Suite. Google Meet supports up to 100 video callers with the free version and up to 250 participants with a G Suite license. We'll explore Google Meet's valuable online meeting features in this chapter.

Google Duo: Duo is a one-on-one video calling app for mobile phones and computers. Designed for consumer users, it's similar to Apple's FaceTime.

Google Voice: Google Voice is a Voice over IP (VoIP) telephone service for both home and business phone calls. It provides a phone number to send and receive calls from any device with an internet connection. Google Voice is sold as an add-on to the G Suite.

Next, we'll take a closer look at the specific features and benefits of each service.

Google Chat

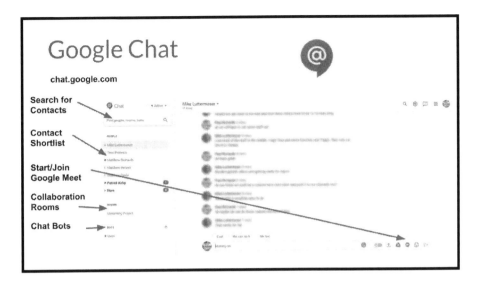

Google Chat is included with every G Suite account and is Google's main instant messaging service. Free Gmail users can chat with the contacts they've added to the service using Chat. Additionally, Chat provides an upgraded experience for G Suite users with all of the instant messaging and group discussion features built into Gmail, plus the added feature, "Rooms." The dedicated chat function is nested in the Gmail interface, but it can also be found at **chat.google.com** where you can chat with contacts and turn your chats into a voice or video call with Meet.

Chat supports inter-organizational communication between work teams. Team members create groups of people, invite members to participate, and send messages to one another Creating groups is an easy way to facilitate team collaboration. Chat integrates directly with Google Drive allowing teams to easily share pictures and documents within the interface. Powerful drive integrations allow users to click the **Drive** button to search shared files and share them.

Google Chat also enables users to create virtual rooms for each team project that offers the threaded conversation teams use to collaborate. As more teams convene online, video conference calls can help them increase productivity and align on shared goals to push projects forward. Chat's robust integration with the entire G Suite allows users to securely share the documents, files, and ideas that they're working on. Organizations can easily manage projects and search through team discussions using Google Chat.

Chat users can also search chat histories and reference old conversations. You can toggle chat history on and off or delete conversations after a specific period for privacy. You can also block contacts you no longer want to communicate with. Invite from contacts outside of your organization to Chat if they have a Google account by simply typing their email address into the search bar and clicking **Send**. Once they've accepted, you can use Chat and include them in new groups.

Google Meet

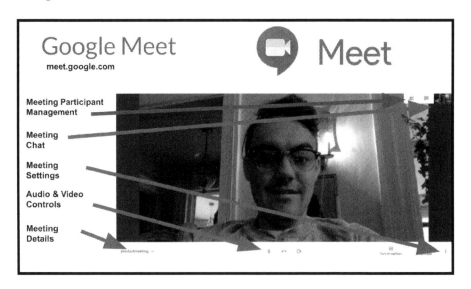

Google Meet is the latest web-based video conferencing application from Google. Meet is capable of hosting meetings for up to 250 participants, and larger meetings when live streaming is enabled for up to 100,000 viewers. Meet features screen-sharing, moderator controls, HD video recordings, and even live captioning.

Google Meet was designed for use directly inside of any web browser. The top right side of the screen offers a feature that enables users to open up a sidebar to view all the participants in the meeting and chat room. Participants with video appear in the center of the screen. The settings area, in the bottom right corner of the screen, allows you to change the meeting layout from a default view to a selection of other viewing options. Google Meet manages and optimizes all aspects of the video conferencing experience.

However, Google Meet also lets hosts control the meeting space by offering a limited set of administrative options. Hosts can invite anyone with an Internet connection and a web browser to a meeting. You can also add people to a meeting from your contact lists in the meeting attendee panel. Another great feature is the ability to call phone numbers directly through Google Meet.

Sharing the Screen

A central feature of online presentations is screen sharing. Users can share their entire desktop, a specific window, or a tab in Chrome by clicking the **Present** button on the bottom right side of the screen.

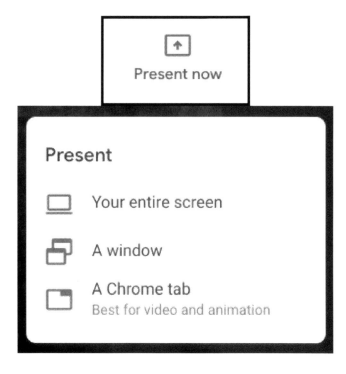

The best option for sharing a video during a meeting is the "Chrome" tab. To use it, simply choose a video from YouTube (or any website) and open it in Google Chrome. Google Meet will give you a list of all tabs open in Chrome to choose from. Chrome tabs used for screen sharing are displayed with a blue box in the Chrome tab. At the top of the Chrome browser, you can click the **Stop** button to end the screen share.

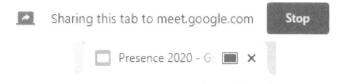

For large meetings, Google Meet features a tiled view of up to 16 participants which you can scroll through in sets of 16. So, if your meeting has 50 participants, scroll through three sets of 16, then view the final two participants on the last screen. For large town hall-style meetings with more than 250 participants, use live streaming, a feature you may add via Google Calendars.

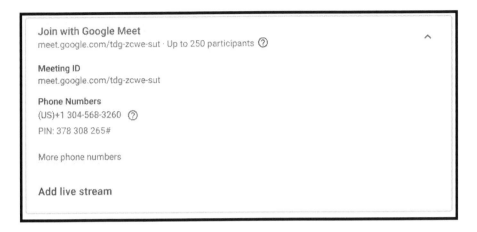

To add a live stream to a Google Meet session, add the live stream as an option inside of the Google Calendar invite. To do this:

1. Schedule a meeting inside Google Calendar.
2. Select **Google Meet** as the video conferencing option. This adds the meeting invitation details to your calendar invitation and opens up an option to "Add live stream."
3. Click **Add live stream** and your Google Calendar invitation will create a link to the live stream that you can share with anyone who wants to watch the meeting.

Advanced Features

Another advanced feature in Meet is a low-light mode that leverages advanced AI technology to sense how your webcam image can be improved. When enabled, the feature automatically decides when to improve the lighting of your webcam. Google Meet also now features automatic background noise cancellation to filter out unwanted noise. The noise-canceling features are ideal for removing the sound of typing on a keyboard or a barking dog in the background.

The Benefits of Google Video Conferencing

Google Meet offers numerous benefits as a solution for online communications. Here's a shortlist:

Accessibility: There are over 1.5 billion active users with Google accounts, so, likely, your friends, family members, and co-workers are already using Google. Moreover, Google services work on all devices and operating systems, including Android, iOS, Windows, and Mac. Meet is perhaps the most accessible video communication tool in the world. It provides numerous features and is easily used inside any web browser – there's no need to download any additional software.

Content: Use Google Meet's recording capabilities to record podcasts, interviews, and online webinars. Invite people by sharing links on social networks or your website. Using Google Meet, you can also live stream to over 100,000 people.

Cost: Google Meet is free for meetings with up to 100 users and the tool built into all G Suite subscriptions. Google Meet is also included with all G Suite subscriptions.

How to Access Google Meet?

The easiest way to access Google Meet is directly through Gmail. Google Meet also features a management dashboard that's available at "meet.google.com." You may access Google Meet via Google Chat, Calendar, and many other relevant locations throughout the G Suite.

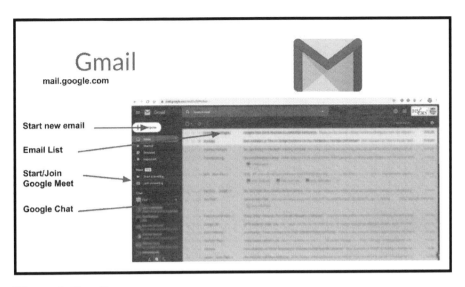

Through Gmail

Gmail is available at "gmail.google.com." Access Meet and Chat on the bottom left side of the Gmail screen. From there, click on contacts to message or call them with the click of a button.

Meet.Google.com

Access Meet by typing "meet.google.com" into your web browser. This page displays all upcoming meetings and allows you to click and join each meeting. It also features a button to launch new meetings instantly.

Messaging with Chat

Easily initiate Meet calls with anyone inside of a Google Chat. Simply click the camera button on top of the Chat message to send a meeting invitation to the person you've selected to enter the meeting.

Making a Video Call

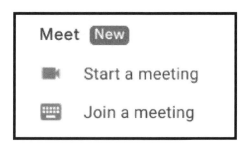

There are multiple ways to start a video call. Most ways to start a Meet call involve clicking a 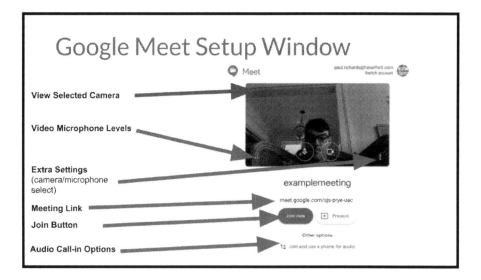 (camera icon) or clicking the **Start a New Meeting** text. Once you start a new meeting, a window opens to invite people to the meeting. When you launch a new video call, a shareable link is created which you can send to other people so they can join the meeting. You can also invite people after a session is started from the meeting attendees' area.

Calendar Integration

Another popular way to create video meetings is through the Google Calendar application. Create a Google Calendar event and then add video conferencing to your meeting with the **Add conferencing** button.

This feature automatically generates a unique meeting invitation inside of a calendar event. This enables you to easily invite people to join your calendar invitation via email.

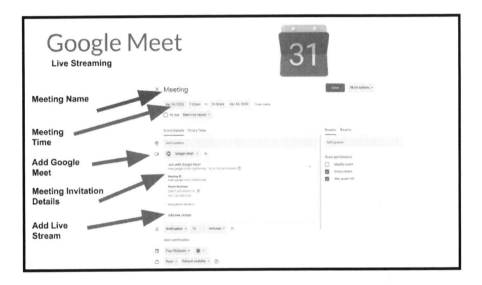

Mobile Apps

Use Google Meet on a mobile phone after downloading the dedicated

app. An ⊕ icon displays on the bottom right of the screen to start new conversations. Tap it to begin a chat or video call. You can also tap

Contacts to view your chat history. To start a video call, click the 🎥 icon on the top right of the screen; video call controls are similar to the desktop chat. The Google Meet smartphone app also enables you to share the screen and send documents.

Getting Started with Google Meet

Few unified communication solutions integrate an entire suite of online tools with phone, chat, and video calling like Google Meet. Instead of buying software for each of these functions, choose G Suite for integrated tools such as Drive, Docs, Sheets, Slides, and more for an all-inclusive experience.

Getting Started

To set up Google Meet on your computer:

1. Create a Gmail account at www.gmail.com. This creates an email address that is used as your Google account to access other services.
2. Log in to your Google account and type "meet.google.com" in the browser. While using the Meet dashboard is ideal, you may also launch video meetings directly through Gmail.
3. View your upcoming meetings and launch new meetings from the Meet dashboard.
4. Chat with your contacts at "chat.google.com" or from inside Gmail at "mail.google.com."

Google Meet

Google Meet is G Suite's video conferencing tool. Over the years, Google merged Google Talk, Google+, Messenger, and Google Voice into a single platform called "Chat." You launch Google Meet from Chat to communicate with anyone using their email address or phone number. Once you've added someone to your contacts, you can communicate with them individually, or in groups with these tools.

Video Conferences

The main function of Meet is video conferencing. With Meet there's no need for participants to download applications or plugins. Users join video conferences by clicking a link which saves time. In just a few clicks, you can email invitations, use calendar integrations from Google Calendar, or use the built-in instant messaging features to join a video conference.

G Suite Integration

Few users are fully aware of everything Google G Suite offers. G Suite's most popular tools are its office productivity solutions: Google Docs, Slides, and Sheets. It's common for users to be familiar with one, but not all. G Suite's integration allows you to schedule meetings with Google Calendars, access chat inside of Google Gmail, and launch meetings from Google Chat. From an administrator's (admin) perspective, user management for the entire online platform takes place from the Admin Console for G Suite.

Free G Suite training is available at https://gsuite.google.com/training/.

The Admin Console

G Suite provides a console for managers and admins to customize the user experience. G Suite Admins access the Admin Console with these steps:

1. Access to the Admin Console is at "admin.google.com." (This is for those with "admin" credentials). Reach out to your IT department if you don't know who your designated admin is. Admins can access individual app controls by clicking "Google Apps" and selecting an app such as "Meet" from the list (controls which only display for Admins).

2. Each Google app features advanced settings that Admins can adjust so entire applications can be enabled or disabled. A radio button displays next to Meet for admins to "Enable Meet."
3. Once Meet is enabled admins must accept the terms and conditions and click "Continue."

Admin Communication Controls

As an administrator, you can manage and control the G Suite. For example, you may:

- Control whether employees can use Chat with people outside of your organization:
- Create an alert for when users try to contact a person outside your domain.
- Allow employees to automatically accept invitations from users within the domain.
- Adjust chat history storage lengths or decide not to save histories.
- Enable or disable video and/or voice calling.

Admin Security Controls

Security settings for the G Suite and Google Meet are "On" by default.

Google pushes security updates to Meet automatically Only those who initiate meetings and calendar owners can mute or remove meeting participants and approve requests to join meetings called by external participants.

Learn more about Google Meet's security here:
https://cloud.google.com/blog/products/g-suite/how-google-meet-keeps-video-conferences-secure.

Most users will never view the Admin Console but reviewing the available control options is a good way for your organization to understand the functionality of this cloud-based workspace. Keep the needs of your organization in mind and change the settings accordingly.

Ensure users get the most out of their G Suite online experience with robust, upfront training. Luckily, Google Docs, Slides, and Sheets look and feel similar to traditional applications. Understanding how these tools relate to one another is critical to the complete adoption of the platform. In cloud-based workspaces like G Suite, most productivity gains will likely come from streamlining workflows and increasing communication capabilities.

For more on training G Suite users, plus training guides and certification opportunities, visit "gsuite.google.com/training" for helpful t.

As a comprehensive, fully featured, and cost-effective solution, the Google Cloud Platform offers many benefits. But it's not the only game in town and it wasn't first to the plate either. That distinction belongs to Microsoft. Next, we'll take a look at Microsoft Teams.

6 MICROSOFT TEAMS

Topic/Feature	Details
Date Launched	Skype for Business replaced Lync in 2015. Microsoft launched in 2017.
Price	Office 365 subscriptions range from $5 to $20 monthly including Teams.
Meeting Participants	Maximum of 250 with the ability to live stream to larger view-only audiences via Microsoft Stream.
Estimated Monthly Users	200 million monthly users and 500k businesses on the platform.
Screen Share	Yes.
Virtual Backgrounds	Yes.
Unique Feature #1	Office 365 Integration and Threaded Conversation style interface
Unique Feature #2	Robust developer platform allows new application integrations.

Microsoft's Windows has evolved to meet the productivity and communications needs of businesses and consumers for decades. Microsoft has been the global leader in operating system (OS) development since the 1980s. Microsoft can offer scalable business solutions that start at the OS found on every computer, except computers that run on Apple's OS. Globally, the Windows operating system is used on nearly 75 percent to 85 percent of computers. This gives Microsoft a competitive advantage in cloud-based communications and workspace solutions.

Over the past decade, Microsoft has leveraged its foothold in the global OS market to launch Microsoft 365, a cloud-based, workplace solution. In 2011, Microsoft placed its popular Office products in the cloud, including Word, Excel, PowerPoint, Visio, and Outlook. Just like Google's G Suite, Office 365's fully cloud-based solution is helping to change the way people work and collaborate. Teams can now work on shared documents in real-time as they collaborate in organized communications channels. As a result, organizations have become more productive, better connected, and workflows more streamlined.

Microsoft Teams is the glue that binds the Office 365 tools together in a collaborative workplace. Teams was designed for online communications with integrations across all the most important aspects of the Office 365 environment. Teams is available on most devices and easily connects users from anywhere in the world whether they're in the office, working from home, or mobile.

One of Teams' flagship features is a threaded conversation function, similar to the collaboration suites Slack and Atlassian's HipChat offer. Teams' chat tool has become a valuable and necessary asset for companies with far-flung global offices and remote employees. Teams' ability to switch between multiple modes of communication make it one of the most popular applications on Office 365.

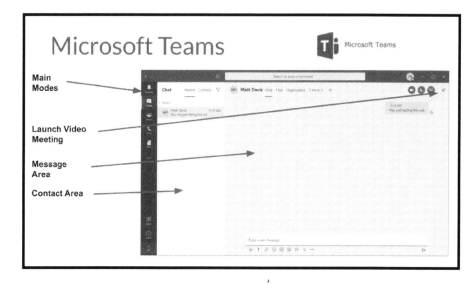

Chat Services

Chat messaging is at the core of Teams. Find **Chat** on the left sidebar button. It allows you to collaborate quickly with individuals or groups of employees by organizing them into a channel to share text, documents, and private files such as images and audio/video calls. Message with people in or outside of your organization securely using the Teams contact list. Organize groups of team members into channels to streamline communications. The interface for Teams is similar to Skype in many ways, making it an easy upgrade path for existing Skype and Skype for Business users.

Notifications

When someone replies to your chat or posts inside of a channel, you're a part of, you receive a notification. User notifications are organized into their tab accessed by clicking the button. Use the activity area to briefly review a news feed of updates for everything going on in Teams. Set up notifications according to your preferences to stay up to date with your team without interrupting your day-to-day workflow. To customize notification settings, click on your profile picture at the top

right corner of Teams and select ⚙ Settings > 🔔 Notifications.
Here's a short list of the notifications that you can adjust:

1. **Banner notifications** display on the side of your computer screen.
2. **Email notifications** appear in your email.
3. **Feed notifications** appear in your activity feed.

In addition to the high-level notification controls, you can also turn off notifications for specific channels and conversations.

- Access channel and conversation-level notification controls via **More options** > **Channel notifications**.
- To hide a channel, click **More options** > **Hide.**

Office 365 Integration

Teams are so much more than a simple chat platform – it's integrated into the most popular Office 365 applications. Users can share Excel, PowerPoint, OneNote, and Word files in the cloud, in real-time. Storing documents on Microsoft's OneDrive is a simple, effective way to provide centralized access to all the files you need to share with team members in your organization.

File sharing and collaboration are the main uses of cloud-based workspaces like the G Suite and Office 365. Microsoft lets users control access to their files on OneDrive. Authors can be sure that all team members have access to the latest versions of their work in real-time. IT managers can set their systems up to keep a copy of important data on the cloud and a local copy on a SharePoint server. Whenever someone makes changes to a file, the software synchronizes it with the previous version and updates it. By integrating with existing services that businesses are invested in, Microsoft provides security for their operations. Microsoft's cloud-based solutions are dynamic in the sense that they help deploy hybrid environments and strategically use both on-premise and cloud-based working environments.

Deploying Microsoft Teams

Microsoft Teams is deployed and scaled quickly in the cloud, unlike traditional video conferencing solutions. By shifting workspaces to the cloud from on-premise solutions, organizations of every size give employees the tools they need to collaborate seamlessly online. With subscription plans ranging from $5 to $20 a month per user, Microsoft's solutions remain competitively affordable. Plus, every Office 365 subscription includes access to Teams. Below is a brief overview of the options available:

Office 365 Plans	Business Basic	Business Standard	Business Premium
Price	$5/User/Month	$12.50/User/Month	$20/User/Month
Exchange	Cloud	Cloud	Cloud
OneDrive	Cloud	Cloud	Cloud
SharePoint	Cloud	Cloud	Cloud
Teams	Cloud	Cloud	Cloud
Word	Web-only	Web & Desktop	Web & Desktop
Excel	Web-only	Web &	Web &

		Desktop	Desktop
PowerPoint	Web-only	Web & Desktop	Web & Desktop
OneNote	Web-only	Web & Desktop	Web & Desktop
Email & Calendar	Yes	Yes	Yes
File Storage	1TB	1TB	1TB
Advanced Security	Yes	Yes	Yes
Advanced Threat Protection	no	no	Yes
PC & Mobile Management	no	no	Yes

*Pricing subject to change. Accurate as of May 2020.

Technical Readiness

Of course, migration to a new platform takes time and requires planning. While the cloud simplifies the deployment of tools in many ways, there are technological and human factors to consider. For example, you'll need to consider network bandwidth and internet access which are required for users to transition smoothly.

Because of these considerations, it's essential to generously estimate the time your employees will need to learn and acclimate to new software.

Poorly planned transitions can negatively impact employee productivity and the efficiency of your business.

Consider unique training strategies for each role in your organization. Microsoft offers a "Microsoft Office 365 Training Center" which is full of resources to assist your employees during the on-boarding process and ensure a smooth transition. Access the Office 365 training center for the U.S. at https://support.office.com/en-us/office-training-center

Think of these resources as deskside support to help you plan training for employees before deploying Office 365. Training will give teams the time to learn about things like new workflows and productivity hacks. As you transition employees to Office 365, take the time to share your implementation vision and explain the benefits of a cloud-based workspace so that everyone understands the technology and is ready to hit the ground running.

Organize Channels

Carefully plan how communications channels for your company should appear inside Teams. Create only as many groups as your company needs to communicate effectively. Each group must include the right people. It's cumbersome to navigate and manage too many communications channels, especially for new employees. Fine-tuning group channels is discussed in greater detail in Part 3 of this book.

Well-planned communication channels reduce the possibility of distractions for specific individuals or teams. To improve collaboration and productivity, I recommend examining the structure of your organization and how it collaborates before you set up channels.

Here are tips for creating communication channels in Teams:

- Understand the internal structure of your company.
- Start small and grow the number of channels as needs come up.

- Determine permissions, administration, and roles before you launch.
- Always keep business objectives in mind.
- Train employees on notification management to allow individuals to tailor and adjust their experience.

Who is Using Teams?

Microsoft says, over 500,000 companies worldwide use Office 365 and that Teams is their fastest-growing software solution. New Teams features include data loss prevention, live captions, live events, whiteboarding, customized backgrounds, information barriers, secure private channels, and intelligent capture. Teams is currently available in 44 languages and Microsoft continues to add more languages to the platform.

Using the Team's Meet Now Feature

Perhaps the easiest way to start a Teams meeting is to use the **Meet Now** buttons integrated throughout the application. You can also find a small video camera/button 📹 , nested underneath the Teams conversation area.

When you click the Meet Now button inside of a specific channel, everyone in that channel is notified. You can also click **Meet Now** inside of a comment. Starting a meeting from inside a comment helps maintain the context of a specific conversation. To do this, click the

← Reply (Reply) button and use the ◻ (Meet Now) button inside of your reply.

After clicking **Meet Now**, a private meeting window opens. Enter a meeting name and then decide to either meet instantly or schedule a meeting for the future.

Once inside a meeting, invite additional people by clicking their names from the suggestion list on the right-side panel. Enter names into the search box to locate people and add them to the meeting. You can also add people from outside of your organization by entering their email or phone number.

Use the link button to copy an invitation link to the meeting that you can send to anyone. By default, members who join from outside the organization are placed in a virtual lobby. When they arrive, their name appears, and you can admit or deny them access by clicking either the 'x' or the checkmark.

Scheduling and Inviting Participants to a Microsoft Teams Meeting

There are a few ways to schedule a meeting with Microsoft Teams. One of the easiest ways is to use the **+ New meeting** button available in the 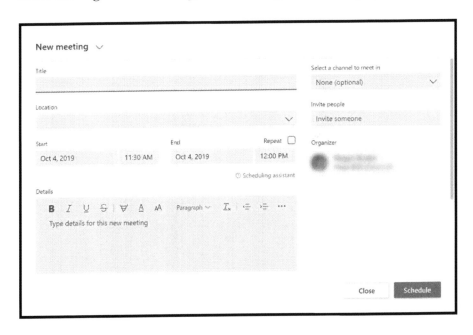(Calendar) tab.

You can also schedule Teams meetings directly through Outlook, Microsoft's email system, or with Exchange, Microsoft's calendaring system. Microsoft's Exchange calendar automatically syncs with the calendar in Teams. Wherever you schedule a meeting, it becomes accessible directly in Teams or the Outlook calendar. To schedule a meeting from the chat window of a Teams channel, select the calendar icon found in the chatbot. The left-hand side of the app also has a calendar icon that you can use to start a New Meeting.

After clicking **New Meeting,** the following window displays.

Here, you name your meeting, invite participants, and select a time. Use the Scheduling Assistant to find a suitable time when all invitees are free to attend.

Note: To view calendar availability with the Scheduling Assistant an invitee must also use Exchange.

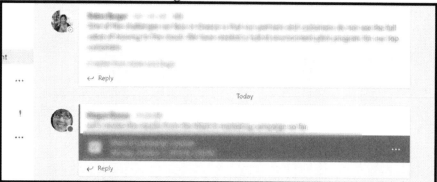

You can also select a channel to automatically invite everyone on a specific Teams channel to a meeting. When you invite an entire channel, everyone on the team will see the meeting in the channels 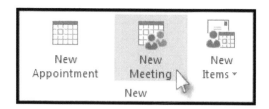 and be able to set meeting agendas, share files, and leave comments on the meeting details. After filling in the meeting details, invite attendees, and click **Save**. Teams will send the notification to every attendee and/or channel with the meeting details.

Schedule Microsoft Teams Meeting from Outlook

You can use Outlook to schedule a meeting from your Inbox or Calendar. Meeting participants can easily accept, enter, or view the Team meetings directly through Outlook.

To schedule a meeting in Outlook, open Outlook and click **New Items** > **Meeting** or use the keyboard shortcut **Ctrl + Shift + Q**. In the next step, you can add people you want to invite.

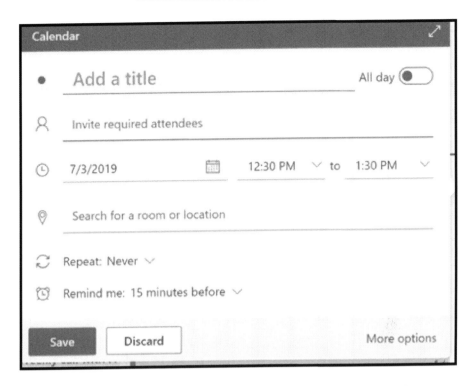

Here you can add a meeting title, invite guests, select a time, and set a location. You can search for rooms or locations to host your meeting. To make the meeting a Teams meeting, click **More Options,** and select the Teams Meeting toggle. All invitees will receive a notification in their inbox. You can also invite people from outside of your organization. You need to provide the email addresses of any outside guests because they don't display automatically like those from inside your organization. After entering the email addresses, click **Add** to send invitations.

Adding Members to Microsoft Meetings

There are several ways to add people to a Teams meeting. For example, if the anonymous "join" option is enabled, you can invite anyone to join the meeting by sending the invitation link. If the "anonymous join" function is disabled, a virtual lobby is set up that requires meeting admission from the host. Teams also allows you to invite people by their phone number and email address. Use the "Invite people" option to invite people before the meeting starts. Or invite people by searching their names, email addresses, or phone numbers in the search box, and then send invitations.

Meeting Controls

Administrators can control various settings such as:

Audio Conferencing

If you have an audio-conferencing license, people can dial into your meetings from more than 90 countries.

Virtual Lobby

People from outside your organization will appear in a virtual lobby. This allows you more control over who can access the conversation and who can't upon entry.

Mute

Mute noisy attendees during a meeting with the mute button For large meetings the muting function is essential.

Screen Sharing

Easily share your screen during a meeting by clicking the centrally located up arrow screen button . Once you click this button, Teams gives you the option to choose your entire desktop, a specific window, or files located on your computer.

Recording Calls

Microsoft Teams allows you to record meetings. To start a recording, click the three dots or **More Options** button and select **Start Recording**. When the meeting is finished, a recording is sent to your inbox.

Zoom video conferencing integration with Microsoft Teams

Microsoft Teams offers developers the ability to build integrations with non-Office 365 products. One of these integrations is a Zoom Video conferencing plug-in which enables users to launch Zoom meetings from inside Teams. By using Zoom with Teams, users can leverage the benefits of Zoom directly within Office 365. Anyone using Office 365 has access to Microsoft Teams for video conferencing. So, you might wonder why you would want to integrate Zoom into your Teams environment? You'll learn about Zoom video conferencing and its many unique features in the next chapter.

Enhancing Productivity

Increased productivity is one of the greatest benefits of video conferencing. You may find that some of the users in your company need more video conferencing features than Teams alone offers. For example, Zoom features webinar solutions to host meetings for thousands of attendees. Zoom also offers the capability of hosting larger meetings up to 1,000 that feature video panelists on screen. These are just some of the reasons that companies may want to integrate Zoom with Teams. The Zoom for Teams plugin is just one of the many integrations available for Teams users.

Conclusion

Microsoft Teams is a powerful application that brings together many of the most important benefits of working online together into a single cohesive application. Microsoft's online workspace bridges traditional popular applications with on-premise solutions in the cloud-like few companies can. Microsoft's Office 365 and Microsoft Teams products together are changing the way millions of people work. In the next chapter, you'll learn about Zoom video conferencing.

7 ZOOM VIDEO CONFERENCING

Topic/Feature:	Details:
Date Started	Founded in 2011 and launched in 2013
Price	Freemium Model puts a 40-minute limit on free users (unlimited 1:1 meetings). Paid plans range from $14.99-19.99.
Meeting Participants	Maximum of 100-300. Varies with a plan (Enterprise supports up to 1,000).
Estimated Monthly Users	300 Million
Breakout Rooms	Yes, paid users can host up to 50 breakout rooms which can be automatically or manually assigned.
Instant Messaging	Chat messaging available in-meetings and in-client
Unique Feature #1	The intuitive control bar is easy to use yet powerful.
Unique Feature #2	Robust security controls, updated after security flaw exposure in Q1 of 2020.

Zoom is one of the leading providers of video conferencing software. Just seven years after the company's 2013 launch, Zoom has become the fastest growing online communications company in the world. With so many features, including a chat interface with cross-platform messaging and best-in-class video conferencing, many are turning to Zoom as their first choice to handle their changing technology needs.

Zoom's popularity comes with good reason first, they back their feature-rich platform with a team of friendly customer service representatives. Eric Yuan the CEO of Zoom, has become an industry thought leader with a mission to "deliver happiness to users." With all of that in mind, Zoom's well-rounded platform has repeatedly been ranked number one in customer reviews on G2Crowd, TrustRadius, and Gartner Peer Insights, among other platforms.

The platform has a lot going for it, it's easy to use and super reliable. Another standout feature is its interface which shows people in little "Brady Bunch" squares, neatly fitting up to 49 people on the same screen. The application is what technical investors call "sticky" meaning users get so attached to using it, they'd never think of switching to another. In this chapter, you will get an in-depth look into everything you need to know to be successful with Zoom.

Let's get started!

Zoom Overview

One look at Zoom's website will tell you how popular the service is. Zoom has testimonials from some of the biggest enterprises in the world, but Zoom's not just for big-name companies, especially following the pandemic of 2020 forcing everyone to work from home. Zoom is now used by small and large businesses alike, as well as nonprofits, governments, institutions, and individuals worldwide, meeting an ever-growing demand for keeping people connected.

What Are the Main Zoom Services?

Zoom's main service is video communications. The interface is simple enough for anyone to understand how to use it in just a few minutes. The application design features a video "front and center" style approach with a single control bar on the bottom.

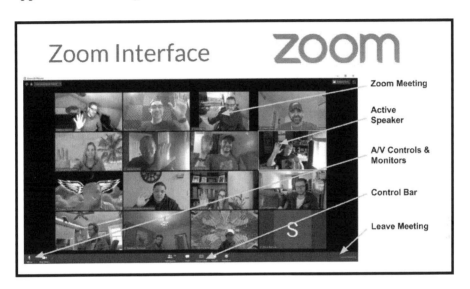

The Zoom meeting control bar features simple icons that represent the microphone control, camera usage, participants, chat, screen sharing, recording, and reaction. Zoom maintains a simplistic and intuitive interface and many of these icons drill down to access deeper levels of control. Under the hood, Zoom offers many video conferencing features that its competitors do not. For this reason, Zoom has become a favorite for power users who host lots of online meetings. Users often choose Zoom for its long list of features, but the true beauty of Zoom is its reliability. People love using Zoom because its purpose-built design works for them 99.99% of the time with no need for IT support. The simplicity of the design makes users feel like they are in control of their meetings.

Zoom's features include:

☐ **Large Meetings:** Support for up to 1,000 video participants on up to 49 videos on-screen at a time, all featuring HD audio and video.

● **Screen Sharing**: Zoom's screen sharing options are organized into **Basic**, **Advanced** and **Files** tabs.

    ○ The Basic tab gives you options to choose any screen on your computer with an option for whiteboards, iPhone/iPads, and any open window.

    ○ The Advanced tab provides access to options for sharing specific sections of your screen, music only or a secondary camera.

    ○ The Files tab will allow you to share specific files from Microsoft OneDrive, Google Drive and Box.

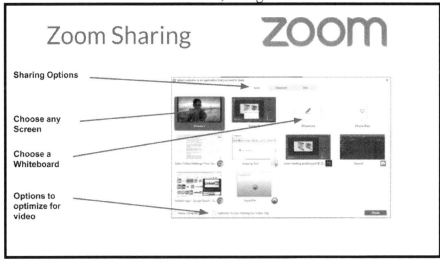

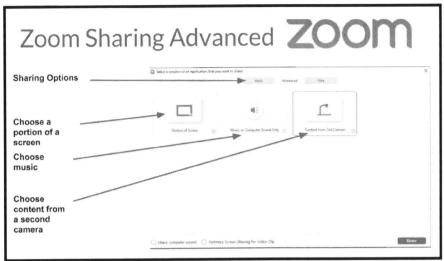

- **Collaboration:** Built-in collaboration tools let participants share screens and whiteboards. Annotation tools add interactivity, so users can make dynamic presentations and explain documents with highlighters and digital ink. Annotation tools display at the top of the screen once a screen share session is in progress.

- **Security:** Zoom offers role-based user security, password protection, participant holds, waiting rooms, and encryption for every meeting. In 2020 a new focus on security made Zoom 5.0 one of the most secure solutions available. Zoom allows all paid users to select where their data is routed with options for selecting servers around the world. Next, a Security button on the meeting control panel gives users quick access features to lock meetings, enable waiting rooms, restrict participant screen sharing, chatting, and renaming themselves. Other meeting security measures such as meeting passwords still need to be set up before the meeting starts.

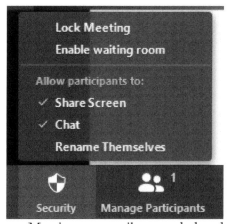

- **Recordings:** Meetings are easily recorded and can be saved to the cloud or locally. Recordings saved in the cloud are referenced using searchable transcripts. Start a recording session by clicking the **Record** button and choosing a storage location. When recording, participants see a red icon on the top left corner of the meeting window. The meeting host pauses or ends the recording from the top left of the screen or inside of the meeting control bar. By default, recorded audio/video files are converted into .mp4 files or the host can also choose to save audio only (.mp4).

- **Calendars:** Streamline scheduling and starting of Zoom meetings from other popular calendar platforms with plug-ins for iCal, Gmail, and Outlook.

Google Calendar Example

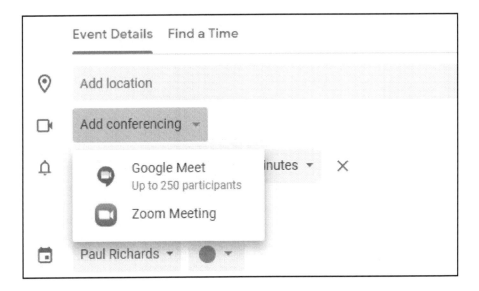

- ☐ **Messaging:** Team Chat lets groups interact with searchable history, file sharing, and a 10-year archive. Convert private chats into video calls with a click of a button.
- ☐ **Zoom Phone**: Zoom phone lets users upgrade a phone call to a meeting seamlessly.
- **Breakout Rooms**: Meeting hosts can organize mini-meetings inside larger meetings by clicking the **Breakout Room** button and selecting the number of rooms and whether to assign participants manually or automatically.

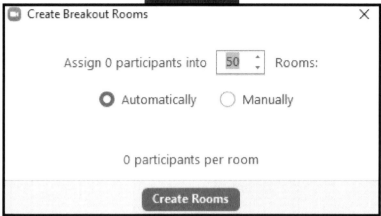

Using Breakout Rooms requires management from a host. See the following table for the current limitations of breakout rooms:

Number of breakout rooms	Max participants in the main meeting*	Max participants in each breakout room
20 breakout rooms	Up to 500 participants	25
30 breakout rooms	Up to 400 participants	13
50 breakout rooms	Up to 200 participants	4

*The large meeting add-on is required for meetings with up to 500 participants.

Now that you're acquainted with Zoom, let's take a closer look.

Online Meetings

With Zoom, you can host online meetings with ease or conduct training and collaborative think-tanks on one seamless platform. Zoom meetings delivers enterprise video conferencing complete with content sharing and unified communications.

The simplified interface is available for use across any device which makes starting and joining meetings a breeze. Zoom also syncs with your calendar system using plugins for Google Calendar and Microsoft Exchange. Zoom has also designed integrations for popular collaboration suites such as Microsoft

Video Webinars

Webinars are excellent for generating leads, conducting training within an organization, and in various other applications. Zoom's facility for webinars is similar to regular Zoom meetings, but with added Q&A features for managing high attendee capacity. Zoom webinars let you host online events with up to 100 *interactive* video participants who can be upgraded from attendee roles to panelist roles who share access to audio and video controls. Or, select a Zoom webinar plan for up to 10,000 *view-only* attendees.

No matter the scale of your webinar, you'll enjoy the easy set-up. When used for sales prospecting, Zoom integrates with marketing platforms to enhance the entire process. Registering is simple too. You can customize and brand your emails and registration forms to flow seamlessly with the rest of your website or organization. Flexible tools like registration management and multiple integration options ensure Zoom connects effortlessly with your CRM. Furthermore, you can even monetize your webinar using PayPal integration with Zapier to manage attendee payment for your webinar.

When it comes time to present, Zoom's webinar controls are both simple and intuitive. Zoom's presentation includes unique, multimedia options, to keep the audience engaged such as private and group chat settings for both attendees and panelists and an area for Q&A and polling with live or text-based answers.

A "hand-raising" feature increases participant engagement by allowing attendees to call your attention when they have questions. The **Attention Indicator** tracks how engaged your audience is throughout the webinar and shows you which viewers are taking the most interest. Since Zoom integrates with CRM solutions like Salesforce, the Attention Indicator proves truly valuable for follow-up after the webinar is complete.

Conference Rooms

"Zoom Rooms" takes video conferencing into the modern era, with an experience designed specifically for online meeting spaces. When it comes to usability, Zoom Rooms tackles the three biggest hurdles people face with virtual conference rooms: booking and starting a meeting, and sharing content. With Zoom's standard features, such as HD video and audio, video conferences go off without a hitch, but Zoom Rooms takes things even further.

Zoom Rooms is designed to provide a control system for your conference room with "One-touch" on a device like an iPad, where one-touch join feature makes getting into a meeting truly simple, and one-click wireless share makes content sharing easy. And, when it comes to bookings, calendar integrations with Exchange, Google Calendar, or Office 365 means participants won't be searching for meeting login details.

To support collaboration, participants can open up to 12 whiteboards at a time with annotation tools to help them work together. Co-annotation added across desktop and mobile devices is stored and can be shared for future reference. At no additional cost, Zoom Rooms also provides digital signage and a scheduling display. Plus, you can simplify your room deployment and with remote management, software provisioning, location hierarchies, role-based administration, and alerts...ultimately reducing your IT costs.

Zoom Phone

Global availability...from almost anywhere is possible using Zoom. Zoom Phone is an enterprise cloud-based phone system that enhances your traditional phone system with additional features for streamlined user experience. Now, escalating a phone call to a video meeting can be done with the click of a button.

Managing users, intelligently monitoring business interactions, and quickly provisioning resources is all made simple thanks to an intuitive and centralized Admin portal. Plus, Zoom Phone is highly reliable and secure, offering high-quality global distribution of HD Voice.

Zoom seeks to be the one unified platform that can manage a whole suite of business responsibilities. Zoom Phone extends these capabilities. Make and receive calls seamlessly while participating in video meetings, sending chat messages, sharing content, and more with Zoom's mobile and desktop applications. Convert phone calls to Zoom Meetings without hanging up. Auto attendants and intelligent call routing make sure calls are connected securely and never missed. Convenient integrations with Microsoft Office 365, Google G-Suite, Salesforce, and others let users experience Zoom while still using their favorite applications.

Zoom Phone also features mail and call recording to allow you to quickly access transcribed messages or calls from any of your devices. Zoom Phone supports your current public switched telephone network (PSTN) service provider from anywhere in the world. Zoom Phone also supports VoIP devices such as those from Yealink and Polycom, among others.

Zoom Chat

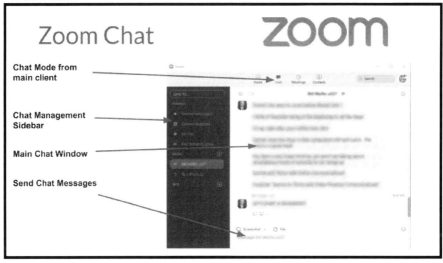

Subscribe to any Zoom plan and Zoom Chat is included with your license. Zoom Chat integrates right into meetings, webinars, and other tools within the Zoom platform. Knowing how to use Zoom Chat makes collaboration easier than ever, whether talking among teams in your organization or bringing in external participants.

With Zoom, file sharing, taking screenshots, using emojis, and searching across contacts, files, and messages is all possible. Calendar integrations sync with contact status to indicate who's busy and who's available (or not), no matter which device they're on; whether desktop or mobile, when they're on or offline--and that's just the beginning.

With Zoom Chat, you can create a virtual workspace and add all the right people for your projects. Enabling file sharing and organized communications without any of the chaos associated with most web chats. Stay focused on the right stuff by starring your channels and contacts, customize your notifications to limit distractions, and organize what's important to you.

How about being able to begin a group video from within a channel or starting a one-on-one meeting with anyone in a chat group. What if the meeting could even scale up to 1,000 people; each equipped with screen sharing and clear-as-a-bell, audio/video capabilities. To start a Zoom chat all you need to do is add contacts to the chat area. Once you've got contacts, off you go.

Wouldn't it be great to be able to search messages for content and links? Zoom's got that. A 10-year message archiving feature prevents accidental deletions. All of this and you can also be confident about security knowing that Zoom encrypts all the data all the time and guards the gates with SSO and multi-factor authentication.

Let's Get You Started with Zoom

Because it's so feature-rich, many new users are intimidated by Zoom. Zoom unifies group messaging, online meetings, and cloud conferencing into one tool. However, while so highly functional, Zoom remains intuitive and simple to use, whether you're on a Windows, Mac, or Chromium Device. Here are the steps to follow to get going with Zoom:

Sign In

After installing the Zoom desktop client for your device, you need to sign in. Yes, you can join a meeting without signing in, with credentials provided in a meeting, but to start or schedule your meeting you will need to sign in.

Sign in options include, using Zoom, Google, or Facebook credentials depending on how you set your account up. You can also use SSO

(Single Sign-On). If you haven't set up a Zoom account, click **Sign Up Free**. If you've forgotten your password, click **Forgot** to reset it.

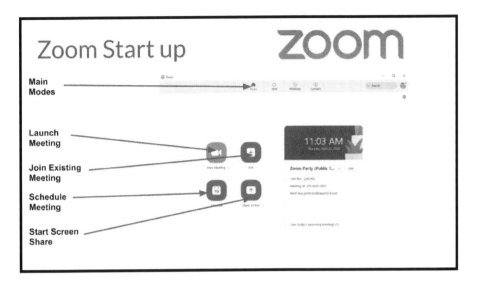

Home

Once you've signed into your account, the **Home** tab displays with the following:

- ☐ **New Meeting**: Instantly start a new meeting with or without video. Click the down arrow to enable video or use your PMI (Personal Meeting ID) to create an instant meeting.
- ☐ **Join**: Join a meeting that's actively in progress or already scheduled with a Meeting ID.
- ☐ **Schedule**: Schedule a future meeting.
- ☐ **Share Screen**: Share your screen in a Zoom Room; with your sharing key or a meeting ID.
- ☐ **Upcoming Meeting**: Indicates the next meeting set for the current day. Add a third-party calendar to sync with your account to see all of your upcoming meetings.

One of the coolest options in Zoom is the ability to change your background image. Just hover over the picture and click on the camera icon to change it.

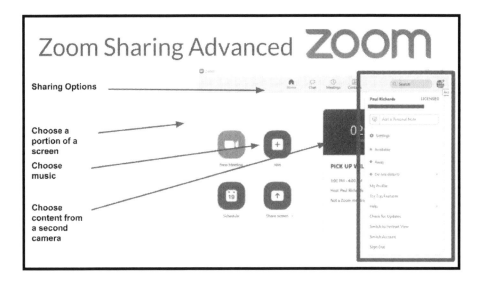

To explore additional options, click on your profile picture for the following features:

- Add a personal note.
- Change your status to **Away, Do Not Disturb**, or **Available**.
- **Upgrade** to Pro (if using a free account).
- **Sign Out** of your account.
- Switch to **Portrait View** for a narrower window.
- Use **Chat**, to view your private conversations with contacts or channels.
- Use **Settings** to change and update settings in the client.
- View **My Profile** tab, you can open the web portal to edit your profile.
- Access **Help**, for assistance from the Zoom Help Center.
- **Check for Updates** to ensure you've the latest version of the Zoom desktop client.

A left side panel on the main Zoom dashboard will open for access to new features depending on which tab you are currently on. The tabs include **Home, Chat, Meetings** and **Contacts**.

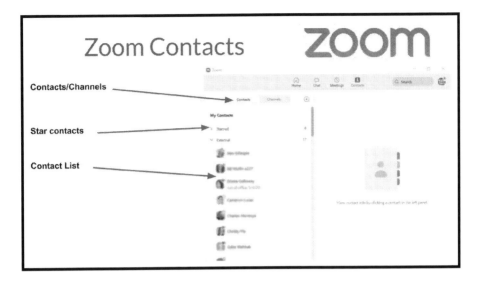

The **Contacts** tabs is a great tool for adding your people to Zoom. Select a contact or channel from the left side panel for the following:

1. **Star**: Star a contact or channel for quick access.
2. **Video**: Click the video icon to begin a meeting with a selected contact, or channel (to invite all its members to your meeting).
3. **New Window**: Hover over a contact or channel name to see and click an icon to open the chat in a new window.
4. **Info**: Additional options for the selected contact or channel with quick access to starred messages, images, and files within the chat.
5. **Message box**: Sends a message to your contact or channel along with code snippets, GIFs, screenshots, or files.
6. **Phone**: Select the **Phone** tab to begin a phone call, view call history, or send voicemail messaging with the Zoom Phone. **Note**: A Zoom Phone license is required to do so.

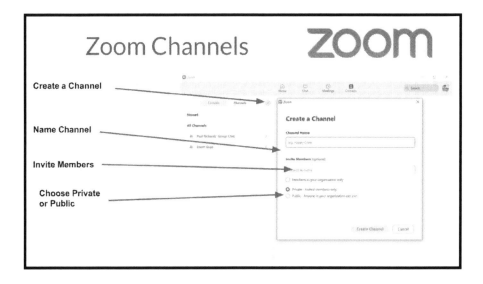

Create channels for collaboration. Channels help you track group projects and are a place to save conversations which can become video meetings. To start a new channel, click the plus button next to **Channels** and fill out the details. Making a channel public allows anyone in your organization to join. Notice each contact has a status icon before their name, letting you know if they're available or not.

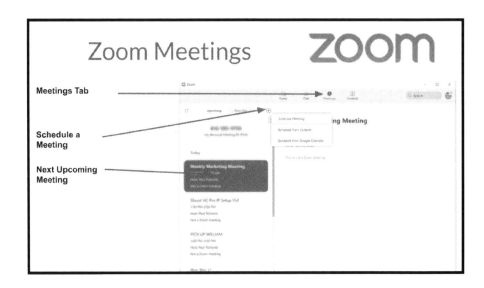

Meetings

After familiarizing yourself with the Zoom dashboard, it's time to head over to the Meetings tab. This is the place to view, start, edit, and delete scheduled meetings.

Select a scheduled meeting to these options in the left side panel:
- **Add**: Click to schedule a new meeting.
- **Refresh**: Click to refresh the meeting list not seeing a scheduled meeting.
- **Start**: Click to start the scheduled meeting selected.
- **Copy Invitation**: Copy the invitation text from a meeting and paste it into an email or instant messenger.
- **Edit**: Edit the options for your scheduled meeting.
- **Delete**: Permanently delete the scheduled meeting.

Scheduling Zoom Meetings

Starting a Zoom meeting is as easy on the spot as it is in advance. Scheduling in advance lets you better manage options and increases security via optional settings like **Recurring**, helpful for weekly check-ins or classes when meets at the same time consistently.

Whether you're using the desktop app, website, or even your mobile app, the process is very

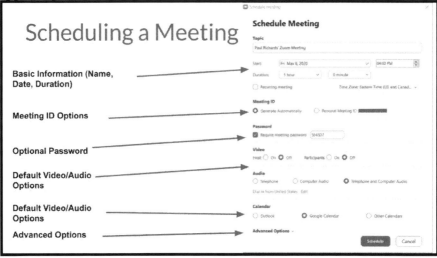

Schedule a Meeting from Your Desktop

The steps to follow to schedule a meeting from your desktop is the same whether using Zoom in your web browser or through a desktop client.

On the Zoom.us website:
1. Click the **Meetings** tab in the Zoom dashboard then click the **+** (plus) button. Optionally you can click the **Schedule** button directly

from the Zoom dashboard.
2. A form opens. Fill in the meeting details, including a date and time. Choose aRecurring meeting or a one-time meeting. Fill out all of the information and click **Save** at the bottom when done.
3. For security consider adding a meeting password. Also, consider some of the Advanced options that can increase your meeting experience.

Advanced Options ⌃

☐ Enable Waiting Room

☑ Enable join before host

☑ Mute participants on entry

☐ Only authenticated users can join: Sign in to Zoom

☐ Automatically record meeting

Alternative hosts:

Example:john@company.com;peter@school.edu

The waiting room feature places new meeting attendees into a waiting room area where they wait until manually admitted into the meeting. You can enable an option to allow participants to join the meeting before the host, mute participants upon entry, and automatically record the meeting.

Personal Meeting Rooms

Your Meeting ID (PMI) is a static meeting ID used to host meetings with people you trust. It's important to guard your PMI because anyone who has it can join your meetings. You'll use the PMI when starting or scheduling meetings. PMI's are ideal for sharing in your email signature. A perfect example of the PMI is when a teacher uses the same PMI each week to meet with students for after-hours teaching sessions. The number is securely shared between students, and used for convenience.

Every Zoom user is also assigned a Personal Meeting Room. One useful tip to make this meeting ID number memorable is to use your 10-digit phone number. This personal meeting room is a virtual space, accessed with your PMI. Your Personal Meeting Room PMI is ideal for back-to-back meetings if the waiting room feature is enabled. This way, you stay in one central Zoom space without having to open and restart every new meeting. With the waiting room feature enabled, continue an existing meeting and let your next meeting attendee enter when you're ready.

If you give someone your PMI link, they can add another person, unless you lock the meeting or use the Waiting Room. Enable "Join Before Host" to allow meeting attendees to join the room before you get there. As you can imagine, freely given PMIs can create some issues and it's one of the biggest mistakes new Zoom users make when planning public or group meetings. Share your PMI with a bunch of people or even on social media... and suddenly anyone with that link can invade their Meeting Room.

 We'll dig into this more later on when we take a closer look at how to control access to your meetings. For now, what you need to know is how to use your PMI when it's appropriate to do so. Most people select a setting to use their PMI to start instant meetings. The other option is to let Zoom generate a random ID. Set Zoom to always use your PMI for instant start meetings, in the Zoom web portal by clicking on your profile photo then clicking **Edit** next to your Meeting ID and checking **Use this ID for instant meetings. Save** your changes and you're done.

What Not to Do with Your PMI

Zoom is a versatile tool that has gained massive popularity as the world demand for high-quality video meeting tools has grown. One particularly fun use case for Zoom is "public events" and large meetings with external guests. Public events invite all sorts of people to join a friendly conversation, watch a movie, jam music, or just share about anything imaginable. In the world of business, public events are also very useful as a tool for building interest among potential clients by inviting them to a live orientation or webinar-type event. When hosting public events, however, be mindful of how you set up the invitations.

Ideally, don't your PMI for such events because too many people will end up having your PMI if you do. Instead, use the option to generate a random meeting ID. It's best practice to use a random ID when:

- Sharing your PMI on social media.
- You aren't yet aware of the best practices of Zoom privacy
- You don't plan on meeting regularly

Fortunately, using a random meeting ID is effortless.

Generating a Random Meeting ID

When setting up a meeting, choose **Meeting ID** and **Generate Automatically** or to use your PMI. In either case, you can require a meeting password as an extra step of security to limit who may join. We will review information about meeting passwords and "two-factor authentication" a bit later.

Inviting Meeting Participants

Whether starting an instant meeting or scheduling one, there are several methods to choose from to invite participants. If you download the Cloud Room Connector add-on, you will be able to invite a room system. Additionally, you can invite by phone if you have an audio-conferencing plan. Without these additional add-ons, you can still use the following options.

Instant Meeting Invites

To start an instant meeting click **Manage Participants** at the bottom of the window, select **Invite** on the panel of participants, and choose from the following options:

Email

Email is a quick and easy option, just select the **Invite by Email** tab and pick an email provider. The default uses the email application on your computer. Alternatively, you can use Google or Yahoo Mail, which will prompt you to sign into your email account.

An email is composed automatically, and all of the meeting information is placed in the body of the email. Just add the recipients and send it out.

Contacts

Click the **Manage Participants** option and go to **Invite** at the bottom of the panel of participants. Click the **Invite by Contacts** tab and select the contact's name from the window. You can also search for a specific contact.

 Click on an individual and their names display a checkmark next to them. They are also added to the list at the top of the window. Click **Invite** in the lower right corner to send the invitations to the selected contacts.

URL / Invitation Text

You can click **Copy URL** or **Copy Invitation** to send instant meeting info anywhere you wish. Copy the meeting join link for easy sharing or copy the full invitation to explain the meeting's details alongside the invitation link. Right-click and select **Paste** or use Ctrl + V on Windows or Cmd + V on a Mac.

Scheduled Meeting Invites

Once you schedule a meeting, you can begin inviting participants. On the desktop client, after scheduling, go to your **Meetings** tab. Select the meeting you want to invite participants to and then click **Copy Invitation**. This copies the meeting invitation so you can paste it anywhere, like into an email or onto a social media page.

Through the web portal, sign in and click **Meetings**. Click on the topic of the meeting and, next to **Time**, you'll see options for adding the meeting to your calendar.

If you select Yahoo Calendar or Google Calendar, it will automatically create an event in your calendar synced with the email service you choose. Click **Outlook Calendar** to generate a .ics file you can import into your Calendar.

You can also manually copy the invitation. Another window opens with the meeting invitation text. Click **Select All** in this window, copy it, and then send it through email or chat.

Joining a Test Meeting

Use Test meetings to try out your setup and get accustomed to Zoom before you're put on a spot in a real meeting. While Zoom is intuitive and easy to use, it's certainly worthwhile to try a test meeting at least once, especially if you want to become a Zoom Pro!

Joining a test meeting is easy. On a mobile device, visit http://zoom.us/test and follow the instructions shown to test your video or audio. Otherwise, visit http://zoom.us/test on your desktop and click the blue **Join** button.

The browser will prompt you to "Open Zoom Meetings." If you do not have the desktop client installed, follow the prompts. When the desktop client is open, a test meeting displays in a pop-up window. This is where to test your speakers for audio output by clicking the **Test Audio** button. If you don't hear a ringtone play use the drop-down menu to switch your speaker selection.

When you hear the ringtone play, click **Yes,** and continue the microphone test. When your microphone is working, you'll hear audio replay through your speakers. If you don't hear a reply, click **No** to switch microphones and repeat the process until you hear the replay. Click **Yes** when you hear the replay.

The next thing to do is click **Join with Computer Audio** to join the test meeting with the microphone and speakers you just tested. You will now be an attendee of the test meeting. This is an excellent opportunity to learn about how attendees see your video feed and to get used to some of the controls.

Of course, your setup might not be perfect at first. In the next section, we'll dive into the details for preparing your audio and video for perfect streaming. Then we'll look at screen sharing and some other features you'll want to take advantage of as you become a Zoom Pro.

Preparing Your Audio

Always test your audio before a meeting. To check your computer's audio, click on the arrow next to the mute icon. This opens up a list of Audio options where you can select **Test Computer Audio** to test your speakers and microphone.

The test will give you the necessary prompts to complete. When finished, simply close the testing window. Zoom works with external speakers and microphones along with headsets.

A simple way to make sure your microphone is working is to look for the green "levels" that display inside of the microphone icon on the lower left of the screen. If a red strike is showing up through the microphone icon, then you are currently muted. Unmute by clicking on the **microphone icon**.

Using Push to Talk

Zoom is filled with features that help make attending and running meetings a breeze, and "Push to Talk" is one feature that helps you avoid unwanted chatter while making sure everyone has an easy, convenient conferencing experience.

Enable the Push to Talk feature to avoid constantly muting or unmuting. To enable it in the desktop client, click on your profile picture and then go to **Settings**. Click the **Audio** tab and check the option to **"Press and hold SPACE key to temporarily unmute yourself." Save** your settings. With this enabled, you will be muted by default. To talk, you just hold down the space bar.

Troubleshooting Issues

An audio echo is one of the most common audio issues to troubleshoot. An echo is usually due to one of three things:

- Having both computer and telephone audio active

- Having a computer or telephone speakers too close to each other
- Having multiple computers with active audio inside the same room

There can also be audio interference from a bad microphone, speakers being too loud, or an echo cancellation failure (which is a device performance issue). As a host, you can mute an attendee to silence the issue or mute everyone to ensure no interference. The attendee can also mute themselves until they sort out the issue.

Preparing Your Video

A test meeting can test your video. However, beyond ensuring your camera is active, there are also some other details and settings you may want to address.

Rotate Your Camera

For Windows users, the camera may display upside down or sideways. To fix this, rotate the camera in your settings section until it's correctly oriented.

If you find this is an issue before a meeting starts, log in to your Zoom client, click your profile picture, go to **Settings** and then the **Video tab**, hover over your camera's preview, and click **Rotate 90°** until it's oriented correctly.

If you're in a meeting and notice that you need to rotate your camera, click the **arrow** next to **Stop Video** and choose **Video Settings**, hover over your camera's preview, and rotate the camera with the Rotate 90° button until it's oriented correctly.

Use A Virtual Background

Virtual backgrounds allow you to change the setting behind you, which can certainly be fun. This feature works best with even lighting and a green screen behind you. The solid green color from a green screen helps Zoom distinguish between you and your surroundings. However, a solid wall will also work. Using a virtual background is straightforward and simple to set up.

You'll get the best results if you:
- Use a solid background color, preferably green.
- Use an HD webcam.
- Use uniform lighting throughout your space.
- Do not wear clothing that matches your background or virtual background.
- Use a background image with an aspect ratio of 16:9 and a minimum resolution of 1280 by 720 or use a video with a minimum resolution of 360p and a maximum resolution of 1080p.

To enable a Virtual Background, sign into the Zoom web portal, and go to **My Meeting Settings** or **Meeting Settings**. Navigate to the **Virtual Background** option in the **Meeting** tab and verify its enabled. If it's disabled, toggle the **Status** to enable it. If a verification dialog pops up, click **Turn On**.

If the option is grayed out, Virtual Backgrounds may be locked out at the Group or Account level, which means you need to contact your Zoom administrator.

For the setting to take effect, log out of the Zoom Desktop Client and then log back in again. Within the desktop client, click on your profile picture and go to **Settings**. Select Virtual Background and check whether or not you have a green screen. Choose an image to use as your background.

You may need to download the "Smart Virtual Background" package to use a virtual background without a green screen. You'll only need to do this once. To enable it just click the ^ next to **Start/Stop Video** and select **Choose a Virtual Background**.

Touch Up My Appearance

The "Touch Up My Appearance" option puts a soft focus on your video display, helping to present a more polished look by evening out your skin tone on screen. To activate this, login to your Zoom client, go to **Settings,** and then **Video**. Alternatively, during a meeting, click the **arrow** next to the video icon and choose **Video Settings**.

Once you're in the settings dialog, click **Touch Up My Appearance** and check the option to begin displaying touched up video. Zoom will remember your preferences for future meetings, so it will stay active until you turn it off.

Screen Sharing

Share your screen in a meeting by clicking the green **Share Screen** icon in the center of the bottom control bar. While a host doesn't need to give attendee permission to share their screen, they can prevent attendees from screen sharing by changing their settings. Here are some other options you may want to look into when it comes to screen sharing.

Side-by-Side View

When screen sharing, participants can switch to side-by-side mode, which allows them to see both the screen being shared and the Speaker View or Gallery View of participants. In side-by-side mode, you can adjust a separator between the shared screen and video stream(s).

When viewing a screen in a meeting, click **Options** then select **Side-by-Side Mode** to enter this Split Screen. The shared screen displays on the left and the speaker(s) on the right. To leave side-by-side mode, go back to **Options** and uncheck it. The screen being shared takes over the window with the speaker(s) shown along the top.

Annotations

Annotation tools are extremely helpful for hosts and participants, but the first thing you need to do is adjust your settings to enable annotations. As a host, you're in control and can turn annotation capabilities on or off for the participants.

When sharing your screen or opening a whiteboard, you'll see the annotation controls pop up. If they don't, select **View Options** and then select **Annotate**.

Note that the **Select, Spotlight**, and **Save** options are only available to the person sharing the screen or whiteboard. Viewers will not see those options. Below is a description of each annotation tool and option:

- **Mouse:**Turn off annotation tools and redisplay your mouse pointer by clicking the **Mouse** button. It's blue when you're using your mouse pointer and the annotation tools are off.
- **Select**: Use this option to select, move, or resize annotations. Select several annotations by clicking and dragging your mouse over them.
- **Text**: Insert text onto the screen or whiteboard.
- **Draw**: Inset lines, arrows, or shapes onto the screen or whiteboard.
- **Note**: Use this to highlight an area of the shared screen or whiteboard with a semi-transparent square or circle.
- **Stamp**: Insert predefined icons, like a star or check mark.

- **Spotlight / Arrow**: Turn your cursor into an arrow or spotlight.
- **Spotlight**: Display your mouse pointer to participants when sharing your screen or whiteboard to point to things you want participants to pay attention to.
- **Arrow**: Display a small arrow in place of your mouse pointer. Click to insert an arrow that displays your name next to it. Click somewhere else to remove the last arrow you placed.
- **Eraser**: Click and drag to erase annotations.
- **Format**: Change the formatting options for your tools, including line width, font, and color.
- **Undo**: Undo the last annotation.
- **Redo**: Redo the last annotation that you undid.
- **Clear:** Remove all annotations from the screen or whiteboard.
- **Save**: Save all annotations as a screenshot.

Use a Watermark

When sharing your screen, select the **Watermark** feature to superimpose an image onto the shared content and the video of the person sharing the content. Start by logging into the Zoom web portal. Select **Account** and then **Account Settings** and find the **Add watermark** option in the **Meeting** tab to make sure the setting is enabled.

To use a Watermark, schedule a meeting. Go to **Meeting Options** and enable the **Enable watermark when viewing the shared screen** option. If you don't see these options or you're not able to activate them, you'll need to ask your Zoom Administrator to make the changes for you.

With the Watermark, when a participant shares their screen during the meeting, a portion of the email address of the person viewing the content is imposed on the shared content as well as over the active speaker's video. For example, if someone with email testing@myzoommeeting.com is viewing shared content, the word **Testing** is imposed over the video.

Zoom Meeting Controls

There are several controls you should familiarize yourself with to use Zoom effectively. Start by learning the basic controls before looking at some of the more important advanced options you can utilize.

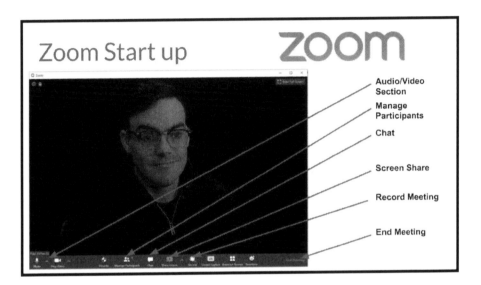

Basic Controls
When participating in or running a Zoom meeting, you'll notice a number of options within the Zoom window. Here's a look at what you can do with them.

- **Mute or Unmute Microphone**: Control audio; when others in the meeting can hear you.
- **Start or Stop Video**: This setting allows you to start or stop your video capture but allows you to remain in a meeting as audio only.
- **Change View**: Use this option to change your video display layout.
- **Speaker**: This option lets you view video of the active speaker.

- **Thumbnail:** This option lets you display the video of the active speaker with other attendees' videos displayed in thumbnails below the active speaker.
- **Gallery:** The display of every meeting attendee in a grid.
- **Camera Control**: Use this to change the PTZ camera settings and presets or to switch to a different camera. This feature is enabled by an administrator. To control the PTZ camera on the far end of a video call, request camera control by right clicking a participant's video.
- **Participants / Manage Participants**: View meeting participants. The host always manages participants.
- **Invite**: Invite Zoom contacts here or invite them using the email, phone, or room system.
- **Start Recording**: Start recording to the cloud or your local drive.
- **Settings**: Use the room passcode to access room settings.
- **Volume Slider**: Adjust the volume of the room's speaker. This resets to default at the end of each meeting.

The Zoom basic controls are used most often and fairly self-explanatory. There are also advanced controls.

Advanced Controls

As with any public gathering, virtual meetings require advanced controls for crowd management. Whether its individuals disrupting the event or solos who managed to find an invite not intended for them, Zoom pros should know how to handle intrusions.

Manage Screen Sharing

Perhaps the biggest mistake new Zoom hosts make is releasing control of their screen. Never let an unknown person in a public event take over your screen or you may end up sharing unwanted content with everyone in the meeting. Always restrict screen sharing before and during the meeting with the host control bar. Select the option to only allow the host to share their screen during a public meeting

Find host controls at the bottom of the window and click the arrow next to **Share Screen**. Under **Advanced Sharing Options**, change **Who can share** to **Only Host**. In your web settings, you can also lock the Screen Share settings to **Only Host** by default for all of your meetings.

Manage Your Participants

Zoom options for public events let you host with full confidence. For instance, you can opt to restrict events so that only signed-in Zoom users can join. When a participant asks to join and they aren't logged into Zoom, they'll see a login prompt. The **Authorized Attendees** setting is another way to control your guest list.

Hosts can lock meetings after all the authorized participants have joined. Think of this as locking your meeting's front door. With a meeting locked, no one else can join, even with a meeting ID and password. To lock a meeting, click **Participants** at the bottom of your window then click the **Lock Meeting** button.

To remove unwanted participants during a meeting, use the **Participants'** menu. Hover over a participant's name and click **Remove** to kick them out of a meeting. Toggle the setting to allow them back in if you accidentally remove the wrong person.

Place an attendee's video and audio connections on hold to temporarily disable them by clicking a participant's video thumbnail and selecting **Start Attendee On Hold** to activate. You can take them off hold when you are ready to have them participate again.

You can similarly disable someone's video or mute them. Participants can be muted one by one, or all at once. Mute Upon Entry is useful to avoid clamor in, particularly large meetings. Select whether you want attendees to be able to unmute themselves or not. For large public meetings, it's helpful to have a co-host to help you manage who gets un-muted using the raise hand feature. Make any meeting attendee a co-host by giving them additional meeting control capabilities from the **Participants** tab.

Hosting a Breakout Session

A breakout room lets you split a Zoom meeting into up to 50 separate sessions. The host of the meeting can choose to split participants into separate sessions manually or automatically and can switch users between sessions at any time. This is a great feature for allowing small teams inside a larger group to have specific conversations outside of the main video conference.

The Zoom Administrator of your account needs to enable Breakout Sessions for users to access this feature. Once enabled, meeting hosts can enable or disable this from the **Breakout Room** button that displays. Meeting hosts can assign participants to specific breakout rooms or make participants co-hosts who can move in-between breakout sessions themselves.

When managing breakout rooms, an important tip is to pre-assign users to specific rooms when scheduling the meeting. Alternatively, set things up so users are assigned automatically. Realize that users within a break room have full audio, video, and screen sharing capabilities.

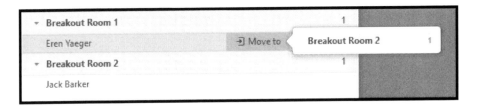

You can set up the following options for your breakout rooms.

- **Automatically move participants into breakout rooms**. Check this option to automatically move participants into breakout rooms. Without checking it, participants need to click **Join** to be added to a breakout room.
- **Allow participants to return to the main session at any time**. Check this option so participants can choose to move back to the main session with their meeting controls. If you do not check it, they will have to wait for the host to end breakout rooms for everyone.
- **Breakout rooms close automatically after X minutes**. If you check this option, breakout rooms automatically end when the specified time is up.
- **Notify me when the time is up**. Check this option so the host of the meeting is notified when the breakout room time is up. This is a helpful alert if you step away from your meeting.
- **Countdown after closing breakout rooms**: If you check this option, participants are shown a countdown of the remaining time until the breakout rooms will end and they are returned to the main session.

When managing breakout rooms, an important tip is to pre-assign users to specific rooms when scheduling the meeting. Alternatively, set things up so users are assigned automatically. Realize that users within a break room have full audio, video, and screen sharing capabilities.

Distraction Management

Zoom features in-meeting chat and private messaging for meeting participants. These can both be toggled on and off to prevent distractions and ensure no one gets unwanted messages during a meeting.

Another option you'll want to be familiar with as a host is the ability to turn off file transfer. While in-meeting transfers can be helpful by allowing users to share files via in-meeting chat, toggling it off prevents users from being bombarded with GIFs, memes, and unsolicited content.

Disable annotation, which allows attendees to doodle and mark up content during screen share, when needed to prevent people from writing all over the screen.

Conclusion:

Zoom's become a leader in video communications because their tool is easy to use, and that's a major feat considering how many advanced features are built into their service. Zoom continues to enjoy incredible growth and its product truly leads the way forward for the industry. While Zoom doesn't offer the integrated online workspace solutions of Google and Microsoft, it's superior performance for video conferencing makes it a must-have for many professionals. Next, let's take a look at Facebook's new video conferencing features.

8 Facebook

Feature:	Details:
Date Started	Launched in 2004. Started Messenger in 2011.
Price	Free product, supported by Advertisements.
Meeting Participants	Maximum of 50
Estimated Monthly Users	2.3 billion total users base. 1.3 billion Messenger users.
Screen Sharing	Yes
Instant Messaging	Yes, the service includes file sharing, games, and ability to send money
Unique Feature #1	The largest world user base
Unique Feature #2	Integrated into the world's largest social media network

You could argue Facebook is the single largest platform used for online communications. Facebook originally started as a social networking tool for groups of college students and has since morphed into an all-inclusive online universe. Facebook offers three main solutions relevant to online communications: the social media platform itself, the Facebook Workplace, and Facebook messenger.

Facebook's social media platform has become a phenomenon that has shaped the way our world understands online communications. Facebook has over 2.5 billion active monthly users connecting with friends, family members, and business contacts throughout the world on their platform. Facebook supports sharing digital content in almost every way spanning video, image, emoji, text, live streaming, and more. Facebook's platform is monetized through its advanced advertising solutions that reported revenue of $16.6 billion in 2019.

Facebook's Messenger service has been naturally integrated into its social media platform allowing users to quickly instant message other users they are friends with. Group conversations can be used for small teams to communicate and video calling is available as well. In April of 2020, Facebook announced a new feature for Messenger called Rooms. Rooms is a feature that provides video conferencing experiences for groups up to 50 callers. Facebook's video conferencing solutions also provide simple screen sharing, audio/video controls, and meeting layout formats.

Until April of 2020, Facebook's main focus in the video communications space has been one-way live streaming. After a 2016 launch, Facebook's dominance in the live content delivery market has been rivaled only by Google's YouTube and Amazon's Twitch platform. Facebook developed several innovative features for live and on-demand video such as watch parties and interactive live audience polling. In 2017, the company's founder Mark Zuckerberg called video a "mega-trend" which would be on par with the move to mobile. Zuckerberg has also said Facebook would become a "video first" company in many subsequent interviews.

For some time in between 2016 and 2020, Facebook was viewed as a walled garden when it came to video content in comparison to top competitor YouTube. While YouTube has become the best search engine for video content, Facebook has become the best social media system for video. YouTube is the world's second-largest search engine.

In April of 2020, Facebook announced people would not have to be logged into the platform to watch live and on-demand videos hosted on the platform. This move brings Facebook's video content to viewers without a barrier to entry similar to YouTube. Facebook also announced that it would allow creators to charge viewers for access to exclusive live streams.

Facebook's dominance in the social media space has allowed the company to spread into other areas of online communication easily because the service acts like a central for online activity. Facebook is the world's fourth largest website and in 2019 the average users spent almost one hour everyday on the platform. The lines between consumer and business use on Facebook are also becoming less important.

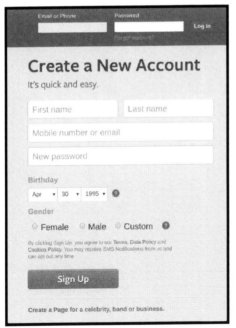

A user may use Facebook to stay connected with friends and family one moment, and then use the same service to connect with business partners over an instant message or video call. Facebook's massive user base makes the tools more effective for communications because so many people are already connected. Facebook also benefits from a familiarity users have with the platform, allowing users to experiment with new services easily (Metev, 2019).

While Facebook remains a very attractive solution for many, it faced unprecedented negative public attention from 2017 to 2019 due to privacy concerns. The company ended up paying a record $5 billion in fees to settle privacy concerns with the FTC (Federal Trade Commission). The allegations cited that Facebook had improperly obtained private information from over 87 million users. Because some of this data was used by advertisers during the 2016 United States Presidential election, the negative press has been estimated to cost Facebook $37 billion (Fortune, Kelleher).

Facebook's Workplace product leverages much of the technology they've developed for public use to give companies a business option and full admin-level controls. The best way to think about Facebook Workplace is a Facebook experience where the only users on the platform are employees of a single organization. The entire Facebook newsfeed is used for company updates, with comments, groups, live streams, instant messaging, and video calling.

While Facebook Workplace does not offer the same type of productivity applications as the G Suite and Office365 it does offer a compelling collaboration space that over 2.5 billion people already know how to use.

So where is Facebook headed? Some would say world domination of online communications. Let's take a quick look at the Facebook Messenger tool to better understand how the private and group communication tool works on the platform. Because Messenger is inside of Facebook, you will need to start by creating an account or logging in with an existing account.

Create an account directly on Facebook.com by filling out the short form. Once you have created an account and gained access to Facebook, connect with other contacts that you wish to communicate with. To find friends you can use the search bar at the top of Facebook.

Type in a friend's name and click the search button . To send someone a friend request, click on their picture to view their profile page. On most profile pages users see an **Add Friend** button at the top of their profile page. The ![Add Friend] button can also display inside of search results. Add Friend may not display on all user accounts depending on individual user privacy settings. Next to the **Add Friend** button are three dots that let you send a message directly or send money. Connecting with someone via Messenger doesn't require being friends on Facebook.

Messenger is nested at the top of the main Facebook application. By clicking the **Messenger Icon** users can easily start new messages with their connected friends and with groups of up to 250 members. Messenger can also be used to host video and audio calls for up to 50 members. Click the **New Group** in the dropdown menu or by clicking the ✏ compose buttons from the messenger dashboard to create one.

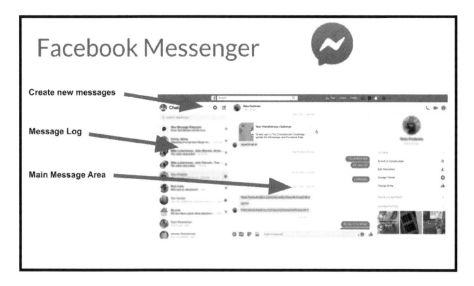

The Messenger dashboard is accessed at
"https://www.facebook.com/messages" or by clicking **See all in
Messengers** on the Messenger dropdown menu. The Messenger
dashboard lists all of your recent conversations on the left side panel.
The center panel is used to display the selected conversation.
Messenger can be used to communicate with others directly or in
groups with a variety of media types. The most common form of
messaging is text messages sent by simply typing into the message area
and pressing enter.

Messenger also offers polls, pictures, games, sending money, voice
messages, gifs, stickers, and files. Polls are a great feature for learning
more about how groups of people feel about a specific question.
Games are an informal way to play with friends from around the world.
Facebook includes Words with Friends, Quiz Planet, Solitaire, and
more. Voice messages are another great way to share media inside of a
private message group. If you're familiar with the Facebook newsfeed,
Messenger includes almost all of the same options for sharing media.

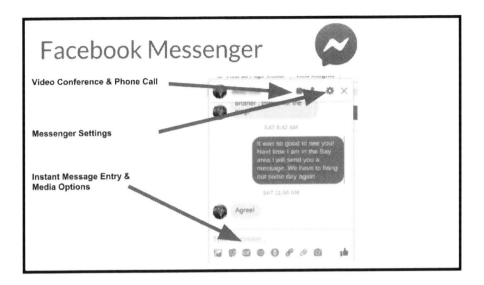

Messenger is built off of Facebook's friend connection system, but you can also message someone without becoming their friend. Messages sent to users who are not already friends show up in an area called "Message Requests." By responding to a message request you're allowing that person to communicate with you, see your status, and know when you have read messages. You can also click a link in the chat box to enable **I don't want to hear from** _____ **to** and permanently block someone from messaging you.

Facebook Mobile View

| Facebook Main Page | Facebook Messenger | Facebook Room |

Over one billion active users of Facebook use it on mobile devices. Facebook positioned access to the Messenger platform in the top right corner of its main mobile app. In a web browser, Messenger is accessed directly through Facebook. On a mobile device, access to Messenger is delivered in a separate app so users can switch between the main Facebook experience and a dedicated, direct communications experience. Having two dedicated applications gives mobile users the ability to go directly to Messenger without opening the main Facebook app.

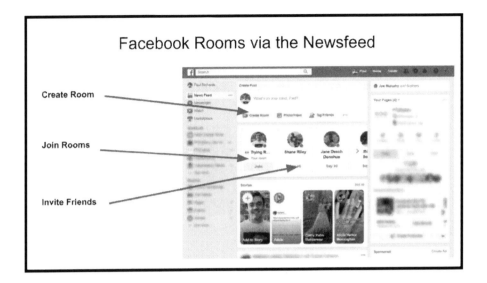

Facebook's latest video communication feature is called Rooms. Rooms are essentially group video and audio chat areas where up to 50 connected friends communicate. As of the publication of this book, Rooms are being rolled out as a feature for Facebook users. Facebook has announced that you can "Create a room right from Messenger or Facebook, and invite anyone to join the video call, even if they don't have a Facebook account. Rooms will soon hold up to 50 people with no time limit." Facebook has also announced functionality to "Start and share rooms on Facebook through News Feed, Groups and Events, so it's easy for people to drop by. "

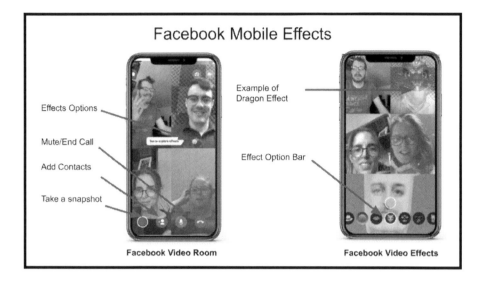

Facebook Rooms has the opportunity to completely change the way video communications happen around the world. Facebook Rooms include the necessities for online meetings such as screen sharing, muting, chat, and two-way communications, but the features that set Rooms apart are designed for consumers.

For example, when joining a room from a mobile device user are prompted to **Tap to explore effects**. While these effects would be inappropriate for a business meeting, they are highly engaging for friends and family in a casual setting. Effects range from augmented reality filters to interactive mini games. An example of this is the basketball mini game that attaches a basketball hoop to your face and drops basketballs from the top of the user's screen. Users can move their heads to catch falling balls and the game keeps track of the score.

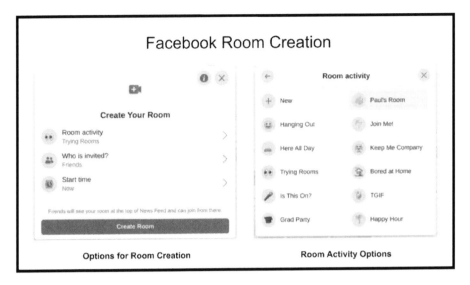

A quick look at Facebook's suggested "Room Activity" options demonstrates some of the popular use cases which include hanging out, grad party, keep me company, bored at home, and happy hour. Once you create a Facebook room, Facebook gives you a link you can share to invite your friends. Facebook can also automate the meeting invitation process allowing you to simply invite all of your Facebook friends or choose specific friends.

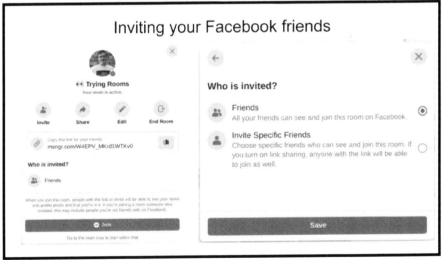

Facebook Rooms Settings & Privacy

From a technical standpoint, Facebook has designed one of the easiest ways to conduct face to face video conferencing. The settings area is simplified into three options: select a camera, a microphone, and an audio output. Next to these options you quickly monitor your microphone levels and choose to play a sample audio clip to test your speakers. At the time of launch, there are six simple keyboard shortcuts. Using the Alt key and a letter key to quickly end a call, enter full-screen mode, share your screen, open the settings, toggle mode, and toggle video.

From a security standpoint, Facebook has designed this tool with three easy to understand security measures. First, Facebook is very clear about who is being automatically invited to your Room. Invite all of your friends or choose specific individuals. Beyond these invitation options, the only way people can find out about your Room is through a secure link that you choose to share. Facebook Rooms also includes a lock room feature, to block any incoming people from joining. Finally, you can also block people from entering your room in the future.

In 2016, Facebook put a "Go Live" button into the hands of billions, completely changing the live streaming and broadcast industry. In 2020, Facebook released a video conferencing solution that is unique in the way it blends social media with online video calling. By allowing users to share video conferencing spaces inside of social media feeds, Facebook automated the invitation process most other video communication solutions required. Similarly, Facebook Rooms can be started in a newsfeed to automatically open invitations to friends in a user's network. Rooms can be started in public groups or events to disseminate invitations even further.

While Messenger remains useful for private messaging and video calls, Facebook's social sharing ability is the reason Rooms is poised to revolutionize video communications. There are few companies in the world with the user base or platform to connect friends, families, peers, and connections the way Facebook can. While Facebook Rooms may seem like a consumer tool, there are numerous business use cases for it as well. Look for updates to this book as Facebook releases enhancements and new features to Rooms.

In the next section, you will learn how to become more productive in online meetings.

PART 3 - Productivity Primer

Chapter 9 - Collaboration, is there a downside?

Not all collaboration is productive. In today's business environment, effective communication and collaboration are valued as key drivers of innovation. On average, in a five-day workweek, employees spend between one to two and a half workdays attending meetings. According to a recent study, employees spend almost 31 hours each month in *unproductive* meetings (HubSpot, 2014). Given these assumptions, most meetings have a 40 percent chance of being unproductive. It's worth noting that an unproductive meeting doesn't mean that the meeting was a complete failure. It just means that most meeting attendees could have been doing something more productive with their time.

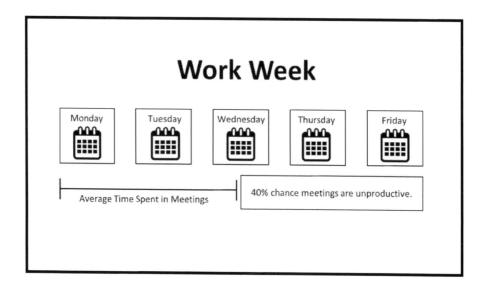

So, how can you prevent employees from spending hours in unproductive meetings? More than likely, most of these meetings should never have been scheduled in the first place. It's practical de rigueur for teams to collaborate at every turn. Frequently, individuals realize only after the fact, that they've wasted valuable time in unproductive meetings with no agenda, action items, or agreed-upon deliverables. A solid agenda is one key to reducing the number of unproductive meetings employees are involved with.

Morten Hanser, the author of *Collaboration: How Leaders Avoid the Traps, Build Common Ground, and Reap Big Results,* promotes what he calls "disciplined collaboration" and describes four types of barriers to collaboration.

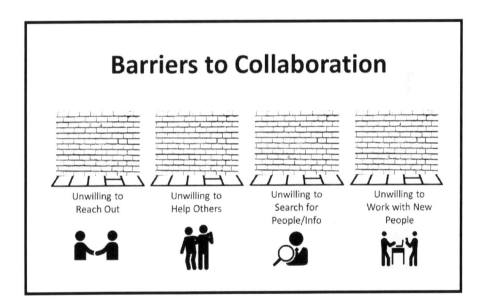

First, Hanser identifies the "not invented here" barrier which describes people who are unwilling to reach out to others. Second, the "hoarding barrier" is where people are simply unwilling to help others. Third, is what's known as the "searching barrier" in which people are unable to find the experts or information they are searching for. Finally, the "transfer barrier" is where people are unwilling to work with those they don't know.

Good managers should do research to determine when the barriers to effective collaboration are too high for the successful completion of a project. When managers suggest that small groups of subject matter experts collaborate, they should consider the three steps of disciplined collaboration Hanser writes about in *Collaboration*.

The three steps are:

1. Evaluate opportunities for collaboration
2. Spot barriers to collaboration
3. Tailor collaboration solutions

Good managers *help* their teams identify opportunities for collaboration. Managers need to mentor their teams to help them gain a working knowledge of how to effectively use available collaboration tools to tailor custom collaboration solutions which current employee workflows and whether they can be optimized.

While there are many collaboration suites and tools available today, none come with a custom execution plan that's tailored to your specific business needs. Hanser rightly points out that "the solution is not to get people to collaborate more, but to get the right people to collaborate on the right projects." This is a process that requires guidance and management to focus on the progress of a specific group within the company.

Most internal collaborations can benefit from management matchmaking. Managers spot opportunities for collaboration, identify barriers and facilitate introductions by using appropriate communication channels, such as Slack, Teams, or other internal platforms. The match-making process works well for large companies with managers who have P&L responsibility and are incented for collaborations that deliver actionable results. Beware, setting up too many collaboration channels can become overwhelming and counterproductive. In an upcoming chapter, you'll learn how to optimize communications channels and head off potential issues.

Businesses can benefit from collaboration with external partners as well. External business partnerships are an effective tool for business development, but they are generally more difficult to establish than internal collaboration projects. Some business-to-business (B2B) partnerships are beneficial. For example, one business specializes in software and the other specializes in hardware. If both businesses recognize their efforts are complementary, a mutually beneficial partnership can be formed.

When seeking a B2B partnership, it's important to start by cultivating a personal relationship with a contact inside the prospective business you wish to work with. These contacts are usually found on the business development or marketing teams of the companies with which you wish to partner. LinkedIn and other professional networks are valuable resources for connecting with potential business development and marketing contacts. When you choose potential companies to partner with, research the company's core values and make sure they align with your firm's values and mission. Look for ways that you can help one another for a mutually beneficial relationship.

Whenever two businesses decide to partner, it's important to clearly define roles and responsibilities. During the early stages of negotiations, it's okay to keep things informal, as you progress, look for opportunities to better define the responsibilities on both sides of the partnership. Then, draw up an agreement that clarifies roles and responsibilities in writing. In today's quickly changing global business world, external business partnerships and alliances have become one of the most important tools to maintain a competitive edge.

It's easy to overstate the benefits of collaboration. Managers should only encourage collaboration when there's a high probability of productive value. Do give teams the freedom to manage the tools and channels that best suit their needs within reason. Managers also need to watch out for the perils of "over-collaboration" where teams underestimate the opportunity costs of collaboration. An opportunity cost is essentially the loss of potential gains that you might have derived from alternative projects. After all, online collaboration is a means to an end, and that end is increased productivity. Promoting disciplined collaboration can help leaders determine whether projects that are heavy on collaboration are effective for their organization. This vision will help leaders identify potential barriers to team collaboration and help them propose solutions to remove those barriers.

Chapter 10: Four Strategies for Hosting Productive Online Meetings

#1: Are you prepared for the meeting?

The first strategy for hosting productive online meetings is simply preparation. Being prepared is perhaps the most powerful strategy for hosting productive meetings. Preparation enables you to come to the meeting confident in your ability to communicate with the online meeting tools available. As a meeting host, you can show all attendees that you're present and paying attention simply by turning on your video camera. The concept of "presence" is used throughout online communications to bring remote teams together. Many people feel uncomfortable on camera yet overcoming this fear as a leader allows you to lead by example.

Why is the use of video so important to hosting productive online meetings? Ninety-three percent of communication is non-verbal, so naturally promoting the use of video cameras during your meetings will increase your communication effectiveness and participant engagement. As an effective meeting host, you need to be mindful of participant concerns about online meeting technology.

Confronting and overcoming any fears you may have using online communication tools is generally the first step you can take toward hosting a productive online meeting. As culture shifts, meeting online will become more commonplace and natural for everyday communications. In a post-COVID world, online meetings have become the norm, replacing in-person meetings by necessity.

In the meantime, meetings with friends and family members online is a great way to help increase your comfort level with technology. Learning to overcome any preconceived notions of discomfort isn't easy for people who have never worked on a distributed team. The first step toward hosting a productive online meeting is breaking the ice and making sure everyone in the meeting is comfortable and ready to proceed in a meaningful discussion.

Test meetings are another great way for managers to encourage employees to gain familiarity and comfort with online meeting platforms. Fun video backgrounds and "Touch up my appearance" features help users become more comfortable with their on-camera appearance. A simple tip for looking more professional is to record a quick video on your preferred meeting platform and watch it to short make adjustments as needed. Lighting, customized backgrounds, and an uncluttered setting can help boost your comfort level.

#2: Create consistency around meetings

As with any meeting, online meetings are more productive if you stick to a consistent schedule. Creating a consistent meeting schedule is a second strategy for hosting more productive meetings. As regularly scheduled meetings evolve, each member of the team can adapt and find their unique role within the meeting. It's important for meeting hosts to arrive at the meeting ahead of time. Think of an online meeting like a gathering of friends at a restaurant. If you arranged the gathering or made the reservation, it's always a good idea to arrive early, ensure a table is ready, and check-in with friends who have arrived early as well. Use the pre-meeting time as a chance to speak with other early arrivals. Teams thrive when professionalism and punctuality are respected at the start.

If you're scheduling a meeting with a new group of people, do your best to set a positive tone for group collaboration. Starting on a high note will help ensure the productivity of future meetings. People look to a meeting host to take responsibility for moving the meeting forward and facilitating input and active participation. It's the host's job to decide when the meeting should start, after a few minutes for casual conversation. If an attendee dominates the conversation, the meeting host may need to intervene to get the group back on track. One discrete way to refocus the meeting is to use a private chat message. Another tactic is to prepare transition or segue questions that can be shared during key points in the conversation.

#3: Create and circulate a meeting agenda and notes

Meetings with a consistent schedule benefit greatly from an established agenda and meeting notes. If someone veers off, the meeting host or co-host can refer back to the meeting agenda. It's commonplace for groups to table or sideline conversation on an issue that goes too far from the intended meeting goal.

Productive meetings have agendas that are distributed in advance and frequently use a shared document for recording meeting notes. If a productive conversation starts to derail the original agenda, a host can make note of the information and table the conversation for review at the next meeting. It's helpful to share meeting notes in an organized folder on a shared drive that all meeting members have access to. Also, posting the notes in a collaboration channel that all members of the meeting are a part of is a great way to keep projects moving forward.

#4: Learn to listen

Learning how to be a good listener is another key to hosting productive meetings. Hosts who do most of the talking need to remember to take a pause, breathe, and listen. A good meeting host will stop and ask for input from other meeting attendees. Transitioning from speaking mode to listening mode is also important for all meeting attendees. Yet, a study from *Psychology Today* finds that only 10 percent of people actively listen during most conversations (Osten, 2016). Sometimes the most important thing you can do is listen.

Listening to and engaging with other meeting participants respectfully and thoughtfully is important. Close listening also can enable you to crowdsource new ideas because we learn from others' experiences. Effective leaders understand the importance of good listening and they enjoy it. Even if you consider yourself the "teacher" in your group, encourage others to interpret and distill the information they've absorbed and shared it during a meeting.

Try a PechaKucha Presentation

Looking for a little inspiration? Try hosting a PechaKucha presentation. PechaKucha, which means "chit-chat" in Japanese, is a way of presenting a story in just 400 seconds with 20 images. Each image receives 20 seconds during the nearly seven-minute presentation. The idea behind PechaKucha is to present critical information as quickly as possible to keep audiences engaged in a storytelling process that they can easily understand.

The PechaKucha presentation format offers a clear beginning, middle, and end to the story. Because each slide is given exactly 20 seconds, the audience knows exactly where they are in the story. This presentation style offers context on presentation length for potentially antsy audiences. PechaKucha imposes order on storytelling and gives the audience a timeline to reference.

While PechaKucha may not be the right choice for every meeting, it demonstrates the power of order in a presentation setting. Besides, an agenda can impose an agreed-upon order that will help meetings stay on track and remain productive. In the next chapter, you'll learn about meeting etiquette and the importance of equity of voice.

Chapter 11 - Video Communication Etiquette

While video conferencing makes remote communication more realistic, tried and true communication practices can help you get the most out of any online communication effort. One strategy for team communication is called "Equity of Voice," in which each member of a meeting is encouraged to have an equal amount of time to speak. Barry Moline, the author of *Connect,* says the secret to powerful connections comes down to four basic communications strategies.

#1: Share personal stories

Sharing personal stories helps individual team members better understand their peers. Personal stories foster the relationship-building process which is foundational to team communication. Spend a few minutes at the beginning of each meeting to help team members build relationships by sharing personal stories. Also, weave personal stories and anecdotes into key points in the meeting where helpful; they can often help reinforce key messages and build retention.

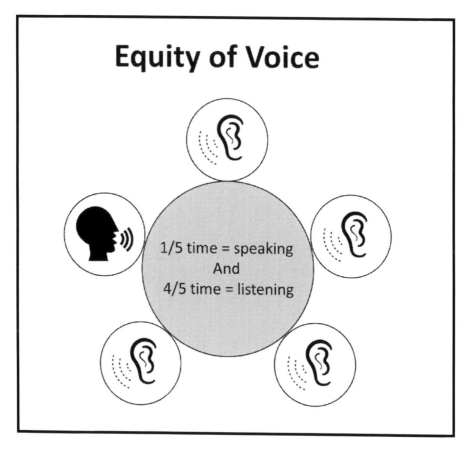

#2: Equity of voice

Achieving equity of voice requires a conscious effort to give each meeting member an equal opportunity to speak during the meeting. For example, in a five-person meeting, each member of the team would speak one-fifth of the time and listen four-fifths of the time. The listening side of the equity of voice is what makes it effective.

#3: Assume positive intent

To help ensure productive meetings, learn how to assume positive intent from others. This assumption helps set the meeting up for success by focusing on what you truly have control over -- yourself. Too often, the "not invented here" barrier and the "transfer barrier" prevent meeting attendees from productive collaboration. Avoid these barriers by encouraging the assumption of positive intent which builds a bridge for communication that might not come naturally.

#4: Value persistence

Anything worthwhile takes time, dedication, and persistence. Once managers identify collaboration projects with significant value to the organization, they need to keep a close eye on team progress and follow-through. Some team members may lose focus, skip important meetings, or come to meetings unprepared. Managers can help by identifying people who can serve as collaboration project leaders. In an upcoming chapter, managers will learn how to use social facilitation to increase productivity and accountability to help employees effectively collaborate on projects.

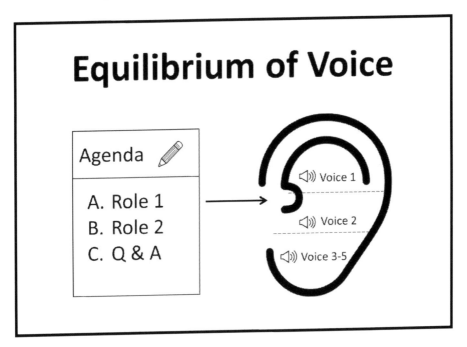

Equilibrium of Voice

Meeting leaders may embrace a new idea I call "Equilibrium of Voice" to push collaboration projects in a positive direction. Equilibrium of voice is a communication strategy that attempts to maximize meeting performance based on goals set in a meeting agenda. A meeting with a perfect equilibrium of voice optimizes the most relevant speakers of a group based on the established agenda and the participants' roles in the overall group. It's almost impossible for meetings to achieve equilibrium of voice without a clear agenda.

Equity of voice can be ideal for team collaboration where an agenda is in the process of being created and individual roles have yet to be defined. During the early stages of collaboration projects, everyone needs to be heard especially during crucial team-building exercises. But once a team has established an agenda, subsequent meetings will benefit from an equilibrium of voice that offers subject matter experts additional focus based on the agreed-upon agenda.

How to get there

Teams can leverage the equilibrium of voice by assuming all team members have positive intent. For example, a thoughtful question may only take a minute to ask but reviewing potential solutions may take a specific team member the majority of a meeting to work through potential answers. Similarly, achieve equilibrium of voice in a webinar-style presentation by offering subject matter experts time to present their ideas before asking questions. Meeting participants can ask questions and receive feedback through the methods decided on the meeting agenda. Meeting hosts should decide ahead of time how to accommodate meeting participant questions and feedback. Subject matter experts are resources that teams rely on to remain informed about subjects they don't have the time to pursue on their own. Meeting leaders need to remember that subject matter experts are an essential element of collaboration.

Create a detailed agenda

Another way to achieve equilibrium of voice is to establish team member roles and align those roles inside of a detailed meeting agenda. Meeting hosts can increase productivity by structuring an agenda that helps all parties understand the roles of team members who have been invited to the meeting. A good meeting host aims to achieve equilibrium of voice between all meeting participants so that everyone can gain the most value out of the meeting.

Employees at all levels of experience need to collaborate and learn from each other. Effective meeting hosts will build break-out sessions into the agenda to help foster new levels of equity of voice between peers. Below is a list of meeting types that are ideal for equity of voice versus equilibrium of voice.

Collaboration Meeting (Equity of Voice)	Presentation Meeting (Equilibrium of Voice)
Team collaboration meeting	Expert webinar presentation
New project brainstorming	Weekly team update meeting
New employee onboarding	Employee performance review meeting
Inter-departmental collaboration	New product launch update
Educational round table	Thought leader fireside chat

Presentation meetings such as webinars, new product launches, and fireside chats, do not require equity of voice because most meeting participants come prepared to learn and absorb new information. Collaboration meetings where teams are brainstorming often benefit from taking the time required to achieve equity of voice for all meeting members. At the core of both strategies, engaged learning is the key to workforce development. In the next chapter, you will learn how to enhance meeting experiences to increase educational and entertainment value.

Chapter 12 - Enhancing the Meeting Experience

Transformational experiences have been studied for many years, especially in the events industry where consumers regularly pay to attend experiential events. Joseph Pine, the author of *The Experience Economy*, writes about the process of capturing attention to cultivate a transformative. The highest level of meeting engagement invokes a transformational experience for attendees. While this may seem like an experience reserved for a weekend of inspirational seminars or a retreat, this chapter will encourage you to think about meetings as mini-transformational opportunities.

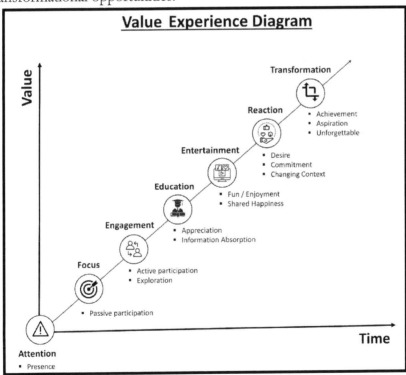

As meeting members spend time together, attention and focus are foundational to engagement. Perhaps the easiest way to conceptualize the idea of invoking engagement in an educational setting is a new term, Edutainment. Edutainment is a process of education that uses entertainment to engage audiences to educate them in the process. This magical intersection between education and entertainment is where meeting participants are inspired to make a change in their own lives. As meetings progress, a good host will encourage engagement and may tailor their approach depending on the type of education that is planned. A good meeting host will plan out simple, but engaging points that have the power to edutain. For example, a short quiz with a funny but relevant question can help to "edutain" an audience.

Most meetings will start with passive participation which can naturally evolve into active participation as the meeting progresses. For example, passive meeting engagement may start with a personal notepad in which attendees write down ideas about questions they may want to ask later in the meeting. Active participation involves asking questions about the content. New collaboration tools can push active engagement to the forefront of meetings with whiteboarding and annotation.

As the educational process in a meeting naturally progresses, a reaction from meeting participants can take multiple forms. A positive reaction from meeting participants involves a feeling of connection and shared vision. Leaders can reinforce a sense of shared vision by the equity of voice inside a team conversation. Another positive reaction is a feeling of inspiration which could lead to an internal commitment to change for the better.

For example, houses of worship may deliver a Sunday service to a large group but afterward break out into smaller groups for spiritual sharing. Inside of these smaller groups meeting attendees can get to know one another better and feel more comfortable opening up. All transformations are personal experiences. Productive meetings can use personalized context to unveil positive reaction opportunities for meeting participants. If a transformation in meeting participants is reached, it will likely include the feeling of achievement and the sharing of aspirations for the future.

This could be described as the "AHA" moment that helps you turn a corner with the help of a new perspective that was shared during the meeting. In an upcoming chapter, you'll learn how social facilitation can be used to share positive feelings and increase an individual's responsibility to perform in a group setting.

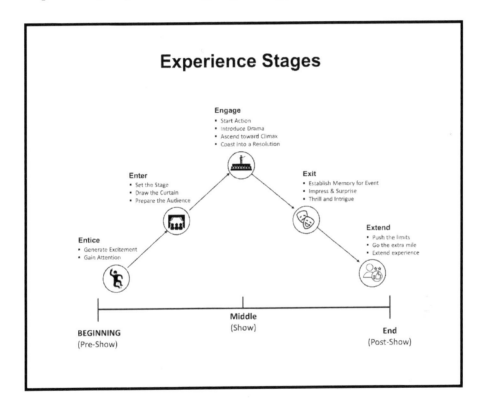

While transformations are highly personal experiences, they are shareable. If meetings take place in a comfortable setting and context, personal experiences can have a significant impact on others when shared. Many people may not feel comfortable sharing their personal experiences in large groups. Consider the use of breakout sessions to break larger groups into smaller, more intimate gatherings.

Structure meetings with a distinct beginning, middle, and end to facilitate the possibility of transformation. The beginning of a meeting starts long before everyone gets together for a video conference. The official beginning of a meeting starts with the meeting invitation to all participants. The invitation is your opportunity to entice meeting participants with an exciting agenda and set the tone for the meeting.

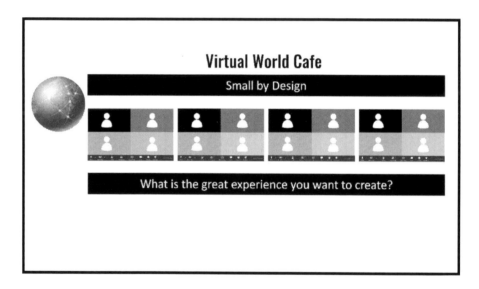

One exercise that's used in many virtual events is called the "Virtual World Cafe" which breaks large meetings down into smaller groups of four people. The idea is to have one meeting host who can have three people join them in a set number of rounds. The idea is a little bit like speed dating in groups. Every 15 to 20 minutes three meeting attendees are rotated between new break out-groups. The host of each small group is responsible for sharing the most powerful ideas from their previous world cafe experience. This way, new people can meet in small groups, and the best ideas are continually shared from past meetings.

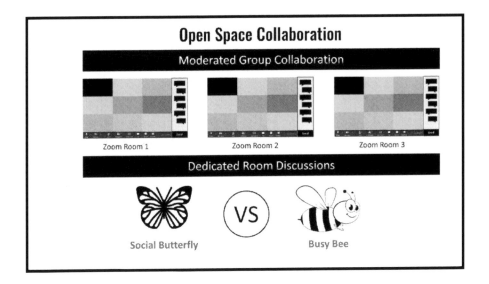

Another popular collaboration meeting experience is called "Open Space Collaboration" which is an organization of multiple independent meeting spaces that attendees are encouraged to jump between. The idea of having multiple conversations going on at the same time allows participants to join each meeting like a social butterfly or dig into a meeting like a busy bee.

Both collaboration meeting concepts, Virtual World Cafe and Open Space Collaboration, are modeled off of in-person group experiences. As you will already know, reviewing the same weekly or monthly business-related presentation can naturally become boring over time. Trying out new innovative ways to stimulate collaboration is a great way to get groups to use the technology productively. In psychological studies, this is known as the Goldilocks effect.

Gamify it

Many traditionally boring aspects of a business are being reinvented to promote education through entertainment with a process called gamification, a highly effective way to promote active learning through the use of a game. Gamification takes the competitive elements of a play and applies content into a fun activity. For example, large meetings and conferences often utilize live trivia events to promote active learning. Live trivia is a great way to leverage a healthy level of competition during meetings.

Two companies that offer online trivia management systems are Crowdpurr and Kahoot. They can be used to host live voting, quizzes, competitions, and much more. Competition has a motivational influence on people by resetting the way they reference themselves against the larger group. Sales competitions, for example, are a proven tool for motivating sales employees to reach their goals using a reward system.

While gamification and sales competitions may motivate some, Jonah Berger, the author of *Nudge*, notes that "if not carefully designed, social comparisons can lead people to get disheartened, give up and quit." The winner-take-all model can motivate people who have a chance of winning, but it can often leave the rest of the pack behind. Tweak your gamification efforts by breaking up groups of people into smaller breakout session meetings. This way, you can moderate and manage comparison sets that employees use to gauge themselves. The focus should be on healthy competition that encourages productive engagement. Bringing together specific sets of people in small groups helps motivate people to work harder without ostracizing anyone for staying at the bottom of the leaderboard. Peer pressure can be a tool used for good, but it needs to be managed.

Social facilitation helps teams build commitment for shared projects and responsibility for showing up and getting the job done. Berger's research clearly shows that peers can help motivate each other to work harder. The mere presence of peers can make it harder for someone to give up on a project. Managers can leverage the power of group presence with online communication to maintain social facilitation even with far-flung teams spread around the world.

Use a scorecard during meetings to keep teams accountable while keeping the process light and fun. Custom scorecards can be created for managers who work with their teams on specific projects. Managers can use scorecards with five to ten data points to keep track of team goals and organize progress reports that can be shared with online collaboration platforms.

For example, you may archive your meeting notes in a folder on Google Drive or Microsoft OneDrive. Inside of your meeting notes you can include data from your meeting scorecards and reference historical data for learning purposes. Then, when you share your meeting notes using an online collaboration platform such as Google Chat, Discord, Microsoft Teams, or Slack, the information is already organized and ready for collaboration.

You can also streamline collaboration by organizing meeting notes and sharing information in team communication channels. Collaborating efficiently requires an upfront understanding of who may benefit from the collaborations and who may not. Information like meeting notes and scorecards should be shared with stakeholders' managers deem essential to the collaboration process.

Once your meeting is coming to an end, it's ideal to plan a memorable meeting exit. A well-planned "exit strategy" should support or reinforce the goals established by your meeting agenda. The end of the meeting is a great time to give co-workers validation for a job well done. If you have a compelling call to action that you are saving for the end of your presentation, consider revealing it within a specific unified collaboration channel. For example, perhaps you have a blog post that summarizes your thinking on a particular subject you're meeting about. Consider posting a summary in a Slack channel with a link to the entire blog post right after your meeting. For example: "A summary of our findings will be posted in the 'blank' Slack channel. Please feel free to push the conversation forward there if you have additional thoughts over the next couple of days."

Thinking through your exit strategy is a great way to conclude meetings with purpose. Consider promoting forward-thinking ideas that can be used to summarize your meeting's purpose and encourage collaboration on priority projects.

The role of small group meetings

Malcolm Gladwell expanded upon the idea of social facilitation in his book *The Tipping Point* in a few important ways. Gladwell studied Methodism's founder John Wesley, and his 4,000-mile journey over horseback meeting with small groups. Wesley traveled from town to town and stayed in each town long enough "to form the most enthusiastic of his converts into religious societies, which in turn he subdivided into smaller classes of a dozen or so people," according to Gladwell. Each small group was encouraged to attend weekly meetings and live by the strict Methodists standard. Gladwell notes that "Wesley realized that if you wanted to bring about a fundamental change in people's beliefs and behaviors… you needed to create a community around them."

In the next chapter, you'll learn why small groups are so effective for communications and you can learn how to organize your online communication channels.

Chapter 13 - Organizing Collaboration Channels

All businesses are in a constant state of change. In *The Grid*, author Matt Watkinson, explains why the traditional way of studying business as a static system is ineffective. Traditionally Watkinson says that businesses like to "break things down into small pieces, and then study them in isolation." While your organization may see strong results from hosting many small meetings with dedicated teams, it's often difficult for these small groups to see the bigger picture. In reality, all businesses are interconnected systems where one decision affects other areas of the system. Managers need to remain tapped into the collaboration efforts of their team members to look for overarching cause-and-effect scenarios that can result from small team decisions. This is why large "all hands" update meetings are also important for connecting departments under a common vision.

No matter how big or small a meeting is, it's an important exercise to consider the best possible outcome for all parties when you bring people together for a meeting. Once you have an idea of the best possible meeting outcomes you can attempt to crystallize the idea into a presentation slide. High-level presentation slides can prime meeting attendees for the desired meeting outcome. You may decide to display this type of slide at the beginning of a meeting, or toward the last moments of a meeting to share a call to action. You can always download a single slide from PowerPoint or Google Slides as an image. Or, insert a single meeting outcome slide as an attachment on calendar invitations to share a slide that primes attendees for your meeting.

As organizations continue to push the boundaries of collaboration, a sense of "digital saturation" can clutter our lives and reduce productivity. If you've already lost important ideas inside of your online collaboration suite, it's time to organize your team's digital strategy. In the *Tipping Point*, Gladwell reviews a concept in cognitive psychology known as "Channel Capacity" which explains the limit our brains have for categorizing specific channels of information. Tests were conducted using a variety of scenarios to test the ability of human memory to categorize and recall information.

"The Magical Number Seven"

One example comes from Bell Laboratories as it decided how many numbers to include in a standard telephone number. Bell wanted to use more than seven digits but after it tested the memory of hundreds of people, the company found that they had a difficult time remembering number strings beyond seven digits. This famously became known as the "The Magical Number Seven" and it explains why telephone numbers are seven numbers long. Gladwell notes: "As human beings… we can only handle so much information at once. Once we pass a certain boundary, we become overwhelmed…[with] our ability to process raw information." (Gladwell, 2000).

Gladwell also points out that the concept of human channel capacity also applies to social channel capacity. A British anthropologist named Robin Dunbar notes, "One hundred and fifty [people] seems to represent the maximum number of individuals with whom we can have a genuinely social relationship with knowing who they are and how they relate to us."

Gladwell notes that the group size of 150 comes up in history repeatedly as the largest number of people in a group that can be organized and still maintain meaningful relationships.

An interesting example of this comes from a religious group called The Hutterites that has a policy in place to split the size of a colony as soon as it reaches 150. Since the publication of *The Tipping Point*, many businesses have adapted to this model and reduced the size of their organizations into smaller, more meaningful groups. Gore Associates is a company that has used this rule of 150 to manage their company, successfully dividing up divisions into groups of 150 even when their plants are right next door to each other.

Small group meetings and sympathy groups

While large organizations of people can become more efficient by working in smaller groups of 150 or less, small group meetings can also benefit from limiting group size. Human intellectual capacity, which limits our ability to interpret raw data, is different from our emotional capacity, which limits our ability to connect with others. Gladwell cites something psychologists call the "Sympathy Group" to help explain the number of people in our lives we can truly care deeply about.

The research shows that on average, people will list 12 people who they're most connected to. Most people are only able to care deeply about a group of 10 to 15 individuals in their lives. This is similar to the "Magic Number Seven" idea where humans begin to overload their ability to distinguish between too many channels of unique information.

Each member of a collaboration meeting is a channel of unique information that others in the meeting need mental space for. For this reason, creating small collaboration groups helps improve meeting efficiency.

These ideas support the need to streamline the way organizations collaborate by creating only as many unique collaboration channels as are necessary. Managers need to limit collaboration channels to those who can truly benefit from them. Managers should actively seek feedback on the relevancy of communication channels to keep channels productive for the team members who use them.

Communications channels will constantly change, and their relevance to specific employees will change as your business needs evolve. Allowing individual team members, the freedom to mute or snooze channels of communication is a good first step for paring down channels. Managers should always question the need for new channels before they're created. Too many channels can make users confused as to where they should post conversations and collaborate. Pare down to only as many unique channels as necessary to make it obvious where collaboration should happen.

Organizing tools

An organized file-sharing system is a foundation for a productive online workspace. If possible, try limiting any single level of your shared folder organization to no more than is necessary. This way, your team can create folders for each collaboration project inside of an intuitively organized architecture. Teams can save files directly in organized folders and easily recall exactly where specific files should be located.

ONLINE MEETING SURVIVAL GUIDE

For example, save a report and the data the report references inside of the same folder. With modern online workspaces, you can even document together and reference shared folders with hyperlinks. The great thing about cloud-based filing systems is that each file has a hyperlink that can be linked within other documents. When you share a file in a team collaboration channel, that file can also include links to other sources of information that are organized in their respective shared folders.

Meeting notes, for example, can reference scorecards, sales data, or other relevant materials. Whenever your team has a question about the sales from a previous month, finding the data and relevant reports is easy and efficient. Once your team is trained on the way the organization structures the data, searching for information becomes a straight path instead of an exhausting digital maze.

Chapter 14 - Priming for Productive Meetings

There's a process in psychology called "priming" that's helpful in meeting scheduling. Priming is a powerful tool for meeting hosts because it helps to influence the way meeting participants will associate their role in association with the proposed meeting. Research shows that priming can influence someone to walk more slowly by having them read words such as "patient," "polite," or "respectful." So, prime your meeting participants to be excited for an upcoming meeting using words such as "impressive" or "tremendous." Depending on the type of presentation you're planning, consider priming your meeting attendees with a catchy title or an associated image attached to the meeting invitation.

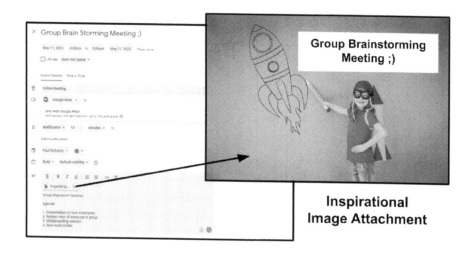

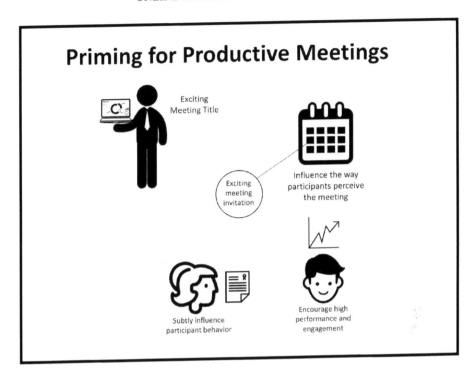

Take a moment to consider the type of priming that would be helpful for your next meeting. As a meeting host, you want to develop a reputation for scheduling engaging and useful meetings. As a meeting participant, you want to participate in thoughtful engagement that provides everyone value, but you also want to defend your own time from unproductive meetings.

The meeting agenda itself is a tool that can be used to prime attendees for a positive experience. The more time you put into the meeting agenda, the more likely your meeting attendees will come prepared to engage. You can brainstorm useful words by searching on Google. Consider searching for "exciting words" or "engaging words" that you can include helping better define the purpose of your next meeting.

Set Yourself up for Meeting Success

Once you have set the stage for your next meeting it is time to make the magic happen. You have already prepared the agenda and your meeting attendees are aware of everyone who is attending. Depending on the type of meeting that you are hosting, you may want to prep key meeting participants with additional information.

Collaboration meetings are generally the easiest to host because the outcome is essentially based on a team sharing ideas to achieve a common goal. Presentation meetings often require more coordination between key subject matter experts and meeting attendees. Meetings that involve subject matter experts sharing content with audiences of more than twenty benefit from an attentive meeting moderator.

Moderators organize questions from an audience and curate audience engagement without disrupting the presenter's train of thought. A simple check-in phone call before the meeting is often enough to prime a key meeting attendee for success. You can also post a poll in a relevant collaboration software channel before a meeting to gauge interest from various parties in your organization. A little research can go a long way toward steering your meeting's agenda and engaging your meeting attendees' interests.

Engaging large audiences is sometimes easier than small group audiences. Jonah Berger, the author of *Invisible Influence,* explores how social influence can affect everything from the products people buy to the satisfaction they feel for their jobs. Berger's research notes that "people don't think they're influenced by others… but ninety-nine-point nine percent of all decisions are shaped by others." Large audiences can be managed carefully using meeting moderation tools to have a positive impact on meeting productivity. For example, large meetings benefit from including questions voiced directly from meeting attendees. Yet, without moderation, most online meetings can be filled with people cutting each other off trying to determine who is supposed to speak next. A good moderator can control the audience's ability to unmute their microphones using the raise hand feature.

Large audiences can enjoy the benefit of shared online spaces for engagement such as chat rooms and break out collaboration areas where positivity can thrive when properly moderated. An active chat room, for example, can spark creative ideas and encourage passive attendees to engage with the activity.

Facilitate positive engagement

Meeting moderators foster positive audience engagement while deterring potentially negative attention as well. One way to foster positive engagement is to come to the meeting prepared with a list of thought-provoking questions. These questions can be entered into the chat room throughout your meeting to encourage engagement throughout your meeting. Consider creating a list of questions that lead up to a climactic "turning point" question. A turning point question assumes your meeting attendees are familiar with the subject matter. Use a turning point question to apply educational subject matter to a real-world situation that applies context to your specific business.

Turning point questions can also be left open-ended. Open-ended questions are a great way to exit a meeting and leave your attendees thinking. Turning point questions that are funny can have a particularly positive effect. Popular memes are a great source for turning point media that can provoke laughter. Memes add entertainment value to make educational content more memorable. A 2019 study found that 74 percent of people send memes to make people smile or laugh and 53 percent send them to react to something. Your organization should have a collaboration system that can be used for communication before and after important meetings. You can recommend that follow-up discussions occur in specific channels on your communication platform. For example, at the end of your meeting, you can say, "let's follow this up with your ideas in the "marketing' channel."

The Cliffhanger Exit

One strategy that encourages productivity after a meeting is a cliffhanger exit. What will surprise us most about this topic at next week's meeting? There is no need to over-think your meeting exit. *The Invisible Influence* notes that "mere exposure [to other people] increases liking." The more you meet with your peers, the stronger your relationships will become. The longer-term your relationship-building efforts are, the less important it is to prepare an amazing exit.

Instead, see if you can develop an inside joke with your team. Great running jokes are open-ended, and they can build team relationships with a simple connection point. Studies show that the more people see something, the more they will like it and familiarity leads to liking. Therefore, simply "Showing Face" and presenting your ideas on any subject should always be considered a benefit for relationship-building. Time is money to many people but perhaps, more importantly, time is an experience that can be shared.

Joseph Pine, the author of the *Experience Economy*, dissects the difference between "time well saved" and "time well spent" to explore the value of shared experiences. Time well saved, is generally associated with hiring someone to perform a service that takes a specialist less time than it would the person hiring them. Time well spent, is associated with more valuable experiences such as team building, events, and vacations that are shared with others. For example, time well saved could be helping someone through a tech support issue. Time well spent, would be collaborating on new use cases for technology that can be applied to business and building a lasting relationship with a coworker in the process.

An interesting aspect of social influence is the ability meeting hosts have to encourage people to perform better as they rally behind an idea. Norman Triplett, the scientist credited with the birth of social psychology, proved this theory by studying competitive cycling.

Triplett's study, which came out in the 1800s, proved that cyclists cycled faster when they raced against a group of other people. His phenomenon is called "social facilitation" and it explains why people perform better in the presence of others. Applying social facilitation to meeting productivity requires an understanding of social influence. It turns out that the presence of others can have a positive or negative effect on performance depending on how complex the task is.

In the 1920s, Stanford professor Bob Zajonc proved that simple tasks like riding a bike generally see improved performance in the presence of others. But, more complex tasks like trigonometry performed in the presence of others will, on average, decrease performance.

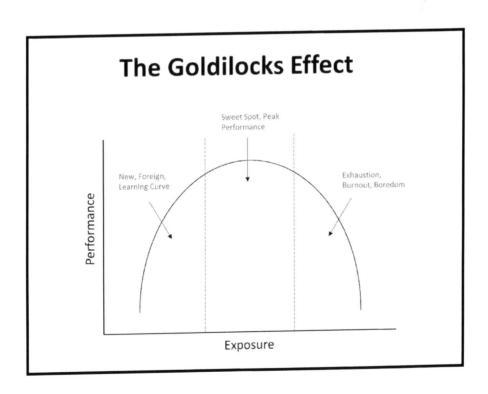

It is possible to increase your influence by simply meeting with people more frequently. The Goldilocks effect may explain why repeated exposure to other people and ideas can increase our affection for them. Repeated exposure to something can help people become more familiar with it. In his book the *Invisible Influence*, Jonah Berger explains how the Goldilocks effect often follows an "inverted U-shape trajectory." This explains why something new is at first foreign, and therefore people initially feel negative toward it. Then, after increased exposure, when things become more familiar, people react positively. At the end of the U-shaped curve, if you have too much exposure to one thing, you may feel bored and again feel negatively toward it. This is the normal Goldilocks-inverted, U-shaped trajectory of affection.

The popular "Death by PowerPoint" saying sums up how many people feel about standard business meetings. Meetings with fresh ideas are more likely to engage an audience. Therefore, it becomes increasingly important to keep your meeting content fresh, the longer you continue to meet with the same audience over time, or you risk losing the interest of your meeting participants.

Think about the beginning stages of the Goldilocks effect of a new boss. At first, your new boss is unfamiliar to you and your experience is mediocre at best. Over time, your boss earns your trust and becomes a leader you look up to. It's possible for great leaders to "buck the trend" and continue to inspire others over a long and successful career. I call this the Goldilocks Extension Process.

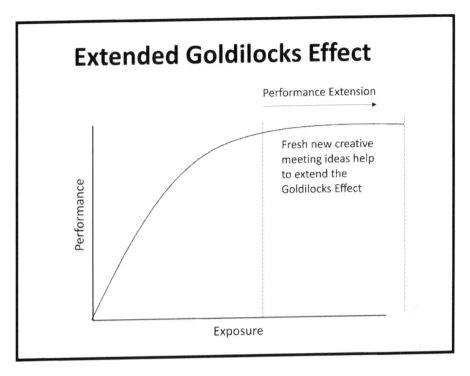

Passion and creativity are tools humans can use to extend the Goldilocks effect and plateau in a productive space. Human relationships are dynamic and online communications give us the ability to easily renew our relationships and collaborate to build deeper connections that can last a lifetime. When teams can overcome challenges together, their relationships grow stronger in a positive way. Extending the goldilocks plateau is when relationships turn in career partnerships that can turn into legacies of teamwork.

Chapter 15: Hosting a Captivating Webinar

At some point in your online communications journey, someone in your organization will want to host a webinar. Webinars are online meetings that feature one or more panelists who make a presentation to a large group. Before you get talked into hosting or joining a webinar ask yourself if a regular meeting format will suffice. Webinars require much less meeting attendee participation than a regular meeting. Therefore, more focused attention on presentation quality is required for webinar hosts. Webinars are often advertised to large audiences and they promise value to the audience in the form of information.

Webinars generally feature a standard hour-long format that easily fits into the schedules of interested parties. It is important to keep in mind that people are busy and will leave a webinar that does not engage their interests within a few minutes. Almost all webinars are recorded and made available for those who registered but didn't make it.

Our team at the StreamGeeks has hosted thousands of webinars over the years. In that time, we have generated powerful educational and entertaining videos that sculpt our online presence. We use the power of social media to distribute our webinars and increase viewership by 10 times. Like most companies, we started our journey into a video by hosting webinars with a simple platform called GoToMeeting. We then moved over to Zoom, which is our platform of choice for video communications.

In our most recent live broadcasts, you will notice that we use Zoom for communications with our live audience. Before we started using Zoom inside of our live broadcasts, our team would live stream directly to YouTube, Facebook, and LinkedIn using software called vMix. Some companies use webinar platforms to generate leads by gating access to the content. While this may seem advantageous, over the long-term, the lack of additional exposure that is gained via social media may wind up becoming a bottleneck for online growth.

We've found a middle ground in which you can use live broadcasting on social media and still offer a gated secure Zoom session for power users. It's much more effective to offer your webinars on social media platforms when your goal is to reach a maximum number of online viewers. In our most recent broadcasts, the use of Zoom meetings as a form of two-way communications inside a larger one-way broadcast has enhanced our story-telling capabilities considerably. It has also created a collaboration space for our audience that includes the important group presence that makes learning experiences come alive.

From the viewer's perspective, it is much easier to watch a webinar on YouTube than on platforms that require a software download. After hosting hundreds of webinars, the data shows that our specific audience prefers the YouTube experience. YouTube can simply sit inside any web browser and can even be played in the background while viewers do other work. Downloading new software for every webinar that someone wants to watch can be cumbersome and may cause friction between you and your viewers.

On the other hand, webinar platforms offer many important features that make them worthwhile for important events. For example, the raise hand feature easily helps webinar moderators find interested participants who want to ask questions. Other Q&A and polling feature truly makes webinar packages designed for high levels of learning and audience engagement. It's worth noting that while webinar software often requires a download, the premium experience is likely to be a more inclusive experience.

At the end of the day, the most important factor for engagement is content. Content is always king. If you have a good pulse on what your audience responds to, you can mine your best content ideas from their questions and turn it into topics for future webinars.

Instead of focusing on up-front lead generation, focus on content and the value you plan to deliver during your webinar. Yes, consider how to educate attendees, but more importantly, ask how you're going to deliver value inside of the time limit set by your webinar. Think about how attendees will spend their time with you. What do you want them to take away from the experience? Ultimately, the more you care about your audience the better you will connect with it.

By increasing your webinar's presentation quality, grow your audience organically. As you continue to create webinars with high presentation quality, the replay value will increase, which will grow your overall audience. You'll start to see viewers commenting on your YouTube videos and sharing them on Facebook and other platforms. An increased focus on the value of your content gives your webinars a longer shelf life. Our team has videos that continue to engage online audiences' years after the webinars were posted on social media.

Depending on how you position your webinar, it can become a great tool for almost any area of an organization's communication plans. Webinars can attract new prospects, engage existing customers, and build relationships in the middle of the sales funnel. When you focus on the quality of your webinar content, your communications goals become much easier to achieve.

Chapter 16: Innovations in Video Communications

Video communications and content delivery technologies have gone through an amazing period of innovation and change over the past decade. Video conferencing technology has moved to the cloud allowing anyone, almost anywhere, to connect and communicate with ease. Live video streaming has made its way into social media putting a "go live" button into the hands of billions of users. This democratization of technology has led to all kinds of new use cases. Throughout this process companies such as Twitch, Facebook, Zoom Video Conferencing, Google, Microsoft, Slack, and Discord have all experienced explosive growth by listening to customers and scaling their offerings to match growing market requirements.

In this chapter, learn about innovations in live streaming, video conferencing, and content delivery. Understanding how to use the latest features in live streaming, video conferencing, social media, and collaboration software will help you design immersive experiences for online attendees. To deploy these software solutions, first think about your event and its relationship to public access. Will your meeting be public, private, or a mix of both?

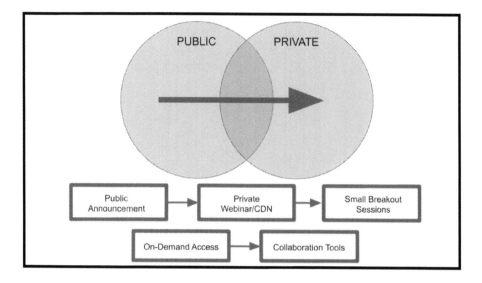

Social media websites - like Facebook Live - are ideal destinations for purely public events because they offer the largest amount of exposure and shareability. However, many meetings are held in a private setting where only specific meeting attendees should have access. Private meetings leverage video conferences and webinars that require unique meeting invitations with optional passwords or webinar registration. Hosting a private webinar or video conference is an easy way to host private presentations that offer user engagement tools in a private setting.

For example, you may host a Zoom meeting with a small group of close friends while a Zoom webinar could host an online event with up to 100 interactive video participants and up to 10,000 view-only. Zoom offers a cloud-based dashboard that provides event managers with a single place to manage registrations and integrations with existing CRM systems. The Zoom webinar system, and most others in the market, offer live Q&A, polling, attendees can raise their hands, and there's even an attention indication feature. For meetings where you want to monetize access, Zoom offers a PayPal integration through a service called Zapier.

One of the most innovative new features announced at the 2019 Zoomtopia conference is live translations. Zoom has supported automatic video transcriptions, a feature that provides speech to text file processing in the cloud, since 2017. The new translation feature provides live translators who can translate your conference in real-time and deliver the translated audio to groups of participants around the world. This new feature allows meeting participants to select their meeting language of choice from a list of available live interpreters. Meeting participants will hear the interpreters at 80 percent audio levels and the original speaker at 20 percent.

Video conferencing industry innovations complement meetings and live streams in many ways. While software like Zoom was not designed for multi-camera video production, it's quite easy to capture a video production system output and use it with Zoom. The easiest way to use video production software and bring it into video conferencing software is through an HDMI to the USB capture card. An HDMI video capture card can bring that video into software like Zoom via the USB webcam and audio inputs. You can also use an external virtual webcam output with many systems as well.

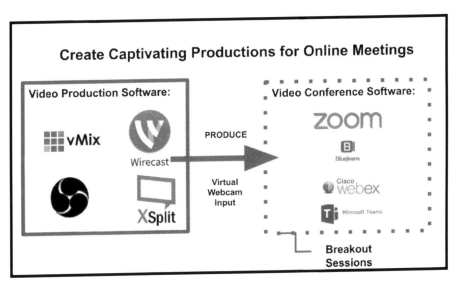

Innovation in the video production industry has also made live streaming and audience engagement easier and more interactive. A company called vMix has developed a tool called vMix social which integrates with Facebook, YouTube, Twitch, Twitter, and IRC to manage comments that are moderated and displayed on-screen. The software provides a dashboard for curated social media comments. It selects the messages that are automatically overlaid on top of the broadcast.

"Data sources" is another powerful feature that makes events more interactive. This feature allows broadcasters to integrate data sources directly into on-screen titles. Information sources can include Google Sheets, Excel, RSS, XML, Text, and more. For example, your live production is underway and there's a title that is automatically updated with timely information via a Google Sheet. The meeting admin only needs to enter information directly into a Google Sheet on their laptop or smartphone to have direct access to the information being displayed on the live stream or inside of the video conference.

Here is another example: A non-profit hosts a live fundraising event and accepts donations via YouTube Super Chat. The super chats (live donations) are logged in a Google Sheet which automatically displays the latest supporters of the project in real-time on the live stream.

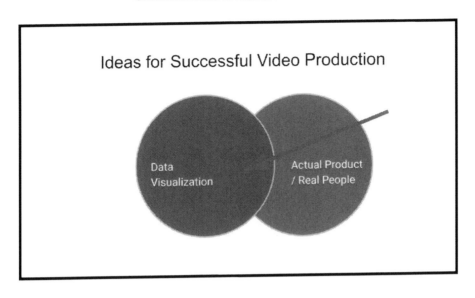

Data visualization and collaboration tools also help educational events find a happy medium between education and entertainment. While charts, graphs, and PowerPoint presentations do a decent job, broadcasters can capture much more audience attention with a mix of data and real-life representations of the data. If you have an app, show the app in detail and share the latest feature. If you sell a product, zoom into the product, and share its look and feel. If you can make your presentation entertaining, you will increase viewer retention. Consider ways to strike a balance between information and entertainment.

One particularly innovative new video production standard is called the NewTek NDI. This technology makes sending and receiving high-quality video sources over a local area network incredibly easy. Software like Wirecast, OBS, vMix, Livestream Studio, and many more all support this standard. The software allows video production companies to do things to connect standard computers to create larger more flexible systems. Along with IP video production, IP connectivity for devices like PTZ cameras allows smaller teams of producers to do more for large events. For example, PTZOptics cameras support the NewTek NDI and have direct PTZ camera control integrations with software such as vMix, Wirecast, OBS, Livestream Studio, and NewTek Tricksters. This enables event managers to use a single ethernet cable to power up a camera (via PoE), receive HD video, and control a PTZ camera.

Note: To learn more about the NewTek NDI or PTZOptics cameras consider taking my free courses available on Udemy at - https://www.udemy.com/course/newtek-ndi/

On the content delivery network (CDN) side, innovations are starting to transform what's possible for event managers. Many CDNs providers now allow broadcasters to monetize their live streams by overlaying instant ads on top of the live video streams. For example, if your favorite soccer player makes an amazing goal, broadcasters can overlay a link for where to buy the player's jersey directly on top of the video player. Twitch takes full advantage of the concept with a feature called "Twitch Extensions," a library of tools that broadcasters can use to overlay interactive elements on top of their video players.

Twitch extensions offer interactive buttons that show additional information about the videogame currently being played. For video games that support this integration, viewers can interact with live elements of the game, such as the player's inventory. PTZOptics has a behind-the-scenes camera control extension that gives the audience control of a PTZ camera. High-profile artists and musicians use this feature to set cameras up backstage and charge live viewers for the capability of controlling the audience's view.

StreamGeeks lives to keep up with all the latest innovations for live streaming, video conferencing, and content delivery. Because technology is constantly changing, I recommend joining the StreamGeeks Facebook Group and following our team on social media.

Chapter 17: Culture Pushes Us Forward

At a high level, it's interesting to look at online communication from a cultural perspective. Human civilization has grown to support massive surging populations. As a result, business and economies have flourished, but traffic and over-population in major cities have become a very real consequence of global growth. For innovative individuals and businesses who want to increase productivity at work but also the quality of life through reduced travel, online communications have become a tool necessary for growth.

The amount of global travel the world supports is astounding. Just take a quick look at a flight radar website to see plane routes on top of plane routes, zipping throughout the world 24 hours a day, 365 days a year. The coronavirus pandemic has put a temporary hold on global travel and given the world a rare chance to gain perspective. The literal roar of the daily hustle and bustle of modern life was reduced to a murmur which allowed us to hear the earth better. Scientists have noted up to a 30 percent decrease in global noise using advanced seismometer machines. Is there something we can learn from the silence?

Ray Oldenburg is a social scientist who can help us understand the importance of public gathering spaces. Oldenburg's work defines an important concept he calls the "Third Place," a social space separated from home and the workplace. Third places are churches, cafes, public parks, and restaurants. The Third-Place idea helps us to better understand the importance of social environments and their impact on our culture. Oldenburg's book, *The Great Good Place*, argues that these third places have the potential to promote a civil society, democracy, and civic engagement. But what happens to a society when our third places are taken away?

Shelter in place orders has forced a virtual third place explosion through pure necessity. Necessity is the mother of invention, and through a vast adoption of technology and internet access, social media, video gaming, and online communications have become the third place. One example of this was the world's largest live concert with over 12 million concurrent viewers that took place in April 2020 inside of a video game. Fortnite, which is one of the world's most popular video games, held a virtual concert with over 10 million viewers in 2019. There's no live concert stadium in the world that could hold even one-tenth of the audience members these concerts are hosting.

The move to esports has also become a global phenomenon for more than just kids playing video games. With sporting events canceled around the world, bike races have continued with network-connected exercise bikes. Major league sports are hosting nationally televised video game versions of scheduled matches. Zoom video conferencing was used during the NFL draft.

Without a doubt, zoom video conferencing became the social media platform of the pandemic. Over 20 million people each day have downloaded the Zoom app, astounding Google, Microsoft, and Facebook which offer similar solutions but aren't seeing the same growth. When the world demanded a space to replace their in-person connections, Zoom became the solution that spread like wildfire.

As of April 2020, Facebook had announced a slew of new features to better accommodate the new virtual third place demand. Facebook said it would upgrade its existing group messaging service to include unlimited free video calling for groups of up to 50 people. Facebook also upgraded its live streaming solution which connects millions every day directly through the social media platform. New features for video communication and live one-way broadcasting will continue to increase online communication in new and innovative ways.

So here we've come to the end together. Whether you'd like to become more productive at work, spend more time doing the things you love, or you have a passion to reduce your carbon footprint, online communications can help you achieve these goals. While the world was headed in this direction slowly, the speed at which online communications are being adopted will help us achieve many great things in a short amount of time. Here's to innovation and human ingenuity! I hope that learning how to maximize the use of the various communications tools discussed in this book has helped you to establish good habits and made you a more productive and passionate member of our increasingly connected global community.

Sincerely,

Paul Richards

paul.richards@streamgeeks.us

ABOUT THE AUTHOR

Paul Richards is the author of "Helping Your Church Live Stream," "The Unofficial Guide to Open Broadcaster Software," and "The Virtual Ticket." Paul is the Chief Streaming Officer at StreamGeeks and also teaches over 30,000 students on Udemy with courses that include live video production, online video communications, and much more.

Sources:

Berger, Jonah. *Invisible Influence*. New York. Simon & Schuster Paperbacks. 2016.

Denis, Metev. How Much Time Do People Spend on Social Media? [63+ Facts to Like, Share and Comment] 2019. https://review42.com/how-much-time-do-people-spend-on-social-media/

Danielle, Abril. Google takes a shot at Zoom by offering free video conferencing https://fortune.com/2020/04/29/google-meet-zoom-free-video-conferencing/

Facebook Rooms. 2020. https://about.fb.com/news/2020/04/introducing-messenger-rooms/

Gladwell, Malcolm. *The Tipping Point*. New York. Back Bay Books. 2002.

Hansen, Morten. *Collaboration*. Boston, MA. Harvard Business School Publishing. 2009.

Hilbert, Martin. Science Magazine. 2011. Retrieved from https://science.sciencemag.org/content/332/6025/60

History of the Internet. Wikipedia. Retrieved from https://en.wikipedia.org/wiki/History_of_the_Internet#cite_note-HilbertLopez2011-14

Kevin Kelleher. Facebooks Parade of Bad News. March 2019. Retrieved from https://fortune.com/2019/03/18/facebook-stock-today/

Moline, Barry. *Connect!*. Outskirts Press, Inc. 2019.

Pink, Daniel. *To Sell Is Human*, New York. Riverhead Books. 2012.

Pine, Joseph. *The Experience Economy*. Boston, MA. Harvard Business Review Press. 2020.

Osten, Caren. Oct, 2016. Are you really listening, or just wanting to talk. Psychology Today. Retrieved from https://www.psychologytoday.com/us/blog/the-right-balance/201610/are-you-really-listening-or-just-waiting-talk.

Online Learning Consortium. Jan, 2018. https://onlinelearningconsortium.org/news_item/new-study-distance-education-overall-enrollments/

Telehealth up 53%, growing faster than any other place of care. AMA. 2020. Retrieved from https://www.ama-assn.org/practice-management/digital/telehealth-53-growing-faster-any-other-place-care

Skype. The History of Skype. 2012. Retrieved from https://blogs.skype.com/wp-content/uploads/2012/08/skype-timeline-v5-2.pdf.

Wainwright, Corey. You're Going to Waste 31 Hours in Meetings This Month https://blog.hubspot.com/marketing/time-wasted-meetings-data. 2014.

YPulse. 3 Stats That Show What Memes Mean to Gen Z & Millennials. Retrieved from: https://www.ypulse.com/article/2019/03/05/3-stats-that-show-what-memes-mean-to-gen-z-millennials/

GLOSSARY OF TERMS

3.5mm Audio Cable: Male to male stereo cable, common in standard audio uses.

4K: A high definition resolution option (3840 x 2160 pixels or 4096 x 2160 pixels)

API [Application Program Interface]: A streaming API is a set of data a social media network uses to transmit on the web in real time. Going live directly from YouTube or Facebook login uses their API.

Bandwidth - The range of frequencies within a given band, in particular that used for transmitting a signal.

Broadcasting - The distribution of audio or video content to a dispersed audience via any electronic mass communications medium.

Broadcast Frame Rates - Used to describe how many frames per second are captured in broadcasting. Common frame rates in broadcast include: **29.97fps and 59.97 fps**.

Capture Card - A device with inputs and outputs that allow a camera to connect to a computer.

Chroma Key - A video effect that allows you to layer images and manipulate color hues [i.e. green screen]

Cloud Based Streaming - Streaming and video production interaction that occurs within the cloud, therefore accessible beyond a single user's computer device.

Color Matching - The process of managing color and lighting settings on multiple cameras to match their appearance.

Community Strategy - The strategy of building one's brand and product recognition by building meaningful relationships with an audience, partner, and clientele base.

Content Delivery Network [CDN] - A network of servers that deliver web based content to an end user.

CPU [Central Processing Unit] Usage - the electronic circuitry within a computer that carries out the instructions of a computer program by performing the basic arithmetic, logical, control and input/output (I/O) operations specified by the instructions.

DAW - Digital Audio Workstation.

DB9 Cable - A common cable connection for camera joystick serial control.

DHCP [Dynamic Host Configuration Protocol] Router - A router with a network management protocol that dynamically sets IP addresses so the server can communicate with its sources.

Encoder - A device or software that converts a piece of code or info to then distribute it.

H.264 & H.265 - Common formats of video recording, compression, and delivery.

HDMI [High Definition Multimedia Interface] - A cable commonly used for transmitting audio/video.

HEVC [High Efficiency Video Coding] - H.264, one of the most common formats of video, MJPEG-H Part 2.

IP [Internet Protocol] Camera/Video - A camera or video source that can send and receive information via a network & internet.

IP Control - The ability to control/connect a camera or device via a network or internet.

Latency - The time it takes between sending a signal and the recipient receiving it. [more]

Live Streaming - The process of sending and receiving audio and or video over the internet.

LAN [Local Area Network] - A network of computers linked together in one location.

Multicorder - A feature of streaming software that allows the user to record raw footage or a camera feed to a file separate from the stream output. [more]

NDI® [Network Device Interface] - Software standard developed by NewTek to enable video-compatible products to communicate, deliver, and receive broadcast quality video in a high quality, low latency manner that is frame-accurate and suitable for switching in a live production environment. [more]

NDI® Camera - A camera that allows you to send and receive video over your LAN.

NDI® | HX - NDI® High Efficiency, optimizes NDI® for limited bandwidth environments.

Network - A digital telecommunications network which allows nodes to share resources. In computer networks, computing devices exchange data with each other using connections between nodes. [more]

NTSC - Video standard used in North America.

OTT Streaming [Over-The-Top] - When a media service bypasses typical media distributors (ie. Facebook, YouTube, Twitch) to distribute content.

PAL - Analog video format commonly used outside of North America.

PCIe Card - Allows high bandwidth communication between a device and the computer's motherboard. [more]

PoE - Power over ethernet.

PTZ - Pan, tilt, zoom.

RS-232 - Serial camera control transmission.

RTMP [Real Time Messaging Protocol] -

RTSP [Real Time Streaming Protocol] - Network control protocol for streaming from one point to point. [more]